Few books on leadership dare to addrak
about the pathological symptoms evidre
shaped more by their culture than by   d
Christlikeness. Healthy and mature ch
leaders, and in one sense, leadership gr   ....urch
growth. *Give Up the Purple* highlights th   ....t unconsciously motivate
many leaders to act in such a way that would damage the church and tries to
address issues in the mission field that are rarely discussed. Reflecting on issues
raised by this book will have a great impact on the future of Christianity in
many regions which are experiencing phenomenal church growth.

Rev Robert Aserian
Iranian Pastor
Head of Leadership Development, Pars Theological Centre

I have thought long and hard about challenges facing leaders in the Majority
World. To my knowledge no one has addressed my concerns and presented
biblically grounded solutions to them as well as Julyan Lidstone has in this
book. Not only does he challenge unbiblical aspects of leadership seen among
Christians today, he also shows how our collectivist culture can harmonize
beautifully with the Bible to forge healthy and dynamic leadership styles which
are both biblically faithful and culturally appropriate.

Ajith Fernando
Teaching Director, Youth for Christ, Sri Lanka
Author, *Discipling in a Multicultural World*

An excellent read! Julyan Lidstone has woven together years of cross-cultural
experience, deep biblical insights, and practical applications. Julyan challenges
and instructs the emerging church across the Muslim world to renounce
patterns of worldly leadership and embrace the counter-cultural example of
Jesus who pioneered and perfected the servant leadership model.

David Garrison
Missionary Author, *A Wind in the House of Islam*
Executive Director, Global Gates

This book is indispensable for anyone who wants to develop biblical leaders. With clarity and insight, Lidstone presents a biblical perspective on leadership in patron-client cultures. Christians have long misunderstood the concept of patronage leadership. *Give Up the Purple* offers not only a clear assessment of the issue, but practical steps for developing biblical leaders in Majority World cultures.

Jayson Georges
Author, *The 3D Gospel*
Editor, HonorShame.com

This book is required reading for anyone who has received the call of God to serve. Whether in the church or in the field, spiritual leadership is crucial to ministry. When a leader fails, or is immature, the consequences are immense; it is not merely someone's hurt feelings on the line, but their eternal life. That said, this book is not a theoretical tome. Through the author's experiences, it instead holds a mirror up to our own selves that are usually hidden away. Reading it will require courage and honesty, but it is in this vulnerable place that we discover our true selves. It is here that we feel the infinite weight of leadership; here that we realize how much courage is needed. The author's quiet but piercing insight offers many salient lessons to Christian leaders of patriarchal cultural backgrounds. Anyone today who dreams of becoming a leader should read it, reflect upon themselves, and ask for the grace of God.

Rev Johnny Jaiheung Song
Executive Director of Mission, Korea Evangelical Holiness Church

What a well-researched, well-written book by Julyan! Leaders around the world are wrestling with such issues as the gospel and culture, while topics such as the decolonization of the gospel are high on many agendas. I believe that *Give Up the Purple* will be an immense help to the global church in navigating some of these complexities. The excellent work done on issues such as power, privilege and patronage add significant depth to the debate. Julyan also does justice to both Scripture and culture, calling us to adopt kingdom values, focusing especially on servant leadership. I want to encourage leaders in all parts of the world to read and discuss this book with their leadership teams, as I think it will contribute greatly towards the acceleration of the gospel in some of the most difficult places.

Peter Tarantal
Advisor, Movement for African National Initiatives Leadership Team
Chair, Majority World Christian Leaders Conversation and
World Evangelical Alliance Mission Commission

Give Up the Purple is a well written and carefully researched book that objects the lofty attitude of the self-idolizing leader who models an authoritarian pursuit of honor, titles and prestige. Instead, it reintroduces the readers to adopt the concept of heathy patronage – a lifestyle that goes back to the biblical root of true servant leadership using Jesus and Paul as ultimate examples of leadership who gave up their "purples." This book helps me to understand the tension of hierarchical cultural and biblical values in leadership that are so evident and pertinent in my culture. It teaches me how a godly patron conducts himself.

Lawrence Tong
International Executive Director, Operation Mobilisation

One often overlooked aspect of honor-shame cultures is the emphasis on hierarchy. Social status and authority go hand in hand. What does the Bible say about leadership in such a context? Julyan Lidstone's *Give Up the Purple* is a thoughtful response to this question. He examines the examples of Jesus and Paul, who depict healthy patronage relationships. Informed by his many years of cross-cultural experience, Lidstone suggests ways to apply Scriptural insights in ministry. This short work promises to catalyze much-needed reflection on a critical topic for the global church.

Jackson Wu
Author, *Reading Romans with Eastern Eyes* and *One Gospel for All Nations*
www.JacksonWu.org

Give Up the Purple

Langham

GLOBAL LIBRARY

Give Up the Purple

A Call for Servant Leadership in Hierarchical Cultures

Julyan Lidstone

Langham

GLOBAL LIBRARY

© 2019 Julyan Lidstone

Published 2019 by Langham Global Library
An imprint of Langham Publishing
www.langhampublishing.org

Langham Publishing and its imprints are a ministry of Langham Partnership

Langham Partnership
PO Box 296, Carlisle, Cumbria, CA3 9WZ, UK
www.langham.org

Isbns:
978-1-78368-681-0 Print
978-1-78368-682-7 Epub
978-1-78368-683-4 Mobi
978-1-78368-684-1 PDF

British Library Cataloguing-in-Publication Data
A catalogue record for this book is available from the British Library

ISBN: 978-1-78368-681-0

Cover & Book Design: projectluz.com

This book is dedicated to my wife Lenna,
my partner in life-long learning,

and to Dr Derek Newton,
my supervisor for the dissertation that gave me the core
argument and insights for the pages that follow.

CONTENTS

Foreword

Some books seem to come to birth in the blink of an eye and with the utmost ease. Others have a long gestation period and a long struggle in the making. *Give Up the Purple* is one of the latter kind, the outcome of many years of friendship with, and ministry among, Muslim men and women, along with deep reflection on the Christian Scriptures.

Julyan Lidstone, and his wife, Lenna, first went to Turkey some forty years ago, and have been immersed in the Muslim world ever since. Turkey may have one foot in Europe as well as one foot in Asia, but scratch the surface and it rapidly becomes very clear that its culture is shaped by its centuries of Islamic heritage along with many features that dominate the Asian world(s). These include a strong focus on shame rather than objective guilt, and assumptions about what a leader looks like, what he is expected to be and do, and how.

Most western traditional theology has read the biblical text through the lens of guilt, and that has formed – often unconsciously – assumptions undergirding the way in which the gospel has been presented by western missionaries wherever they have gone. Undoubtedly the Bible has plenty to say about real guilt, the objective reality of sin, and the grace of God in the atoning death of Christ as the only way to deal with it. But it is easy to be blind in one eye: if you read the Bible through the lens of shame, you find it illuminates so much in both Old and New Testaments, precisely because so many of the cultures into which God's revelation came were shame cultures. We need both lenses.

In any generation, and in any culture, there are specific challenges to the deep transformation of a follower of Jesus. Initial coming to faith is one thing, progressive reconstruction of mind and heart and lived discipleship is another. Nowhere is this more evident than in the patterns of leadership adopted by Christian leaders. Shame cultures create particular problems. Julyan has long been troubled by the results among Muslim background believers. But he would be the first to insist that truly godly leadership is contested in any culture. The issues in shame cultures are different and specific, and he explores and explains some of these, but it would be entirely wrong to imply that in no other context are there also problems and failures. Our human fallenness sadly ensures that radical transformation, and genuine counter-cultural patterns, are painfully absent the world over.

At the 2010 Third Lausanne Congress in Cape Town, from every continent and numerous cultures came the recognition of the sheer urgent need for godly, Christ-like leaders. One section of the Cape Town Commitment spells out both what happens when Christian leaders "use their positions for worldly power, arrogant status or personal enrichment" – that is, when they conform to worldly patterns of leadership – and by contrast the nature of radical, spiritual leadership that embraces the example of Christ. "Authentic Christian leaders must be like Christ in having a servant heart, humility, integrity, purity, lack of greed, prayerfulness, dependence on God's Spirit, and a deep love for people."[1]

Julyan helpfully unpacks for us some of the issues in shame cultures, and in the Muslim world, which make it particularly hard for Christian leaders to embrace a very different way of leading – and for those whom they lead to recognize and welcome it. This is emphatically not a call to embrace western ways or culture, but for us all, together, to seek humbly to "do things the Jesus way." That may lead to misunderstanding, scorn, suffering or rejection; but that was our Lord's experience, too.

In today's highly mobile world, we all rub shoulders with men and women shaped by cultures different from our own. May this book help God's people, wherever they may be, to understand better the worldview of others as well as our own. And may that deeper understanding lead us all to more effective disciple-making, and more godly disciple-living. May we all "Give up the Purple"!

Thank you, Julyan, for writing!

Rose Dowsett
Milngavie, Glasgow, UK

---

1. *The Cape Town Commitment: Part 2*, "Call to Action"; section 11D, 3: "Christ-centred Leaders." The full text of the Commitment is available for free download on www.lausanne.org.

Preface

Healthy, life-giving leadership is the single most important factor for the success of any organization or movement. Too often, when programmes fail, leaders blame their followers. Bosses blame workers for poor results, not seeing their failure to provide a coherent strategy and encouraging environment. Pastors complain that their churches are not growing because of the apathy, laziness or prayerlessness of their members, failing to realize that it is their responsibility to deliver the clarity and training that will secure the wholehearted engagement of their congregations.

For many years, I have been deeply concerned about the way poor leadership hinders the progress of the gospel among the least reached peoples of the world. Domineering, controlling leaders, who take offence when questioned and refuse to delegate authority, cause division, disappointment, defections and burnout. Their actions betray a fundamental misconception that the church belongs to them and is the means for them to gain honour and status. This understanding of leadership is taken from their cultures, and not from the teaching and examples of the Bible. Leadership that is not grounded in the principles and values of Scripture may lead to success in terms of numbers, but it cannot foster true transformation of lives and communities.

However, the New Testament shows us a different way. When Paul and Silas came to Philippi they were welcomed by Lydia, a woman from Thyatira, or Akhisar in modern Turkey (Acts 16:14). She had built a business dealing in purple cloth, which in those days was a luxury item. The purple dye was extracted from thousands of tiny shellfish brought up from the sea, which made it very expensive. Only Roman aristocrats were allowed to wear the purple toga that showed their rank and status. Men competed for the positions that would give them the honour of being entitled to wear it. Paul was dramatically different, for when he was arrested he could have claimed protection as a Roman citizen, but instead willingly forsook that privilege and underwent the humiliation of being stripped and beaten in public (Acts 16:22). He was following his Lord, who "did not regard equality with God as something to be exploited, but emptied himself, taking the form of a slave, . . . he humbled himself, and became obedient to the point of death, even death on a cross" (Phil 2:6–8).

This was what the early church expected of its leaders, that they would not compete to wear the purple of power, pomp and prestige. Instead they would give up wearing the purple, following Jesus who freely and willingly laid aside his glory in order to be crucified, the ultimate disgrace of the punishment for slaves. Jesus's humiliation on the cross brought salvation to mankind; Paul's humiliating beating laid the foundation for the church in Philippi; when Christian leaders humble themselves today the result is life for the church.

I believe the biblical basis for servant leadership makes this message universally applicable. My wife Lenna and I have enjoyed the richness of forty years of ministry among the people of the Middle East, and as much as we have been blessed by friendship with some precious saints, we have also been saddened by the hurt and pain caused by talented and enthusiastic church leaders who misunderstood and misused the authority entrusted to them. Colleagues working in Asia, Africa and Latin America have confirmed that many promising new ventures have stagnated or even been destroyed because of abusive leaders. Here in the West churches suffer when pastors are influenced by corporate models, pushing their own vision and driven to achieve impressive results at the expense of personal vulnerability and community life. These biblical principles even apply to the worlds of business and education. Friends tell me the most common reason that gifted staff move on to other jobs is frustration and dissatisfaction with their boss.

Dysfunctional, toxic leadership is a problem everywhere, and the examples of Jesus and Paul in the New Testament provide the solution that applies to every culture. They show the way to counter-cultural leadership that transforms cultures, creating communities that demonstrate the kingdom of God here on earth.

1

Leadership Problems

Leadership in Honour-Driven Cultures

Ali[1] had always been a leader. He was born to a Muslim family in a Middle Eastern town, and, as the first-born son, he was their pride and joy, often given special treats and favoured over his younger brothers, and especially over his sisters. When he was a boy, the neighbourhood kids looked to him to organize their football games, and at school his teachers gave him the honour of being class president. He was a bright student and did well in the engineering department at university.

Ali had a promising future, but his natural sense of justice was outraged by the brutality of the government, and so he became involved in radical politics and a political party. Again, his natural leadership qualities – intelligence, attractive personality, and ability to take the initiative – drew the attention of the party's leaders and he was asked to organize a demonstration to protest against the blatant corruption of local officials.

A few days later, there was a knock at his door in the middle of the night and three plain clothes policemen handcuffed him, put a bag over his head, roughly bundled him into the back of their car, and took him to the security headquarters. He was locked up in solitary confinement, with loud music playing day and night to keep him awake. Every day, he was blindfolded and interrogated for hours on end. The police wanted to get the names of other opposition activists, and they beat him when he refused to give them the information. Ali was strong and determined and eventually the police let him go. This, however, was just the beginning of his troubles, for he found that he had been expelled from his course, and that his friends no longer wanted to

---

1. Ali is not a real person. I have composed his story based on many true incidents from the lives of people I have known.

1

associate with him. Nightmares and flashbacks deprived him of sleep, and depression dogged him during the day.

Although he had never been a particularly religious person, Ali started to pray, crying out to God for peace of mind and a solution to his problems. One night, he had a vivid dream: a shining figure in white told him that his neighbour, Hossein, had a message from God for him. Ali woke up with a feeling of great excitement and a wonderful sense of joy he had never experienced before. Although it was still very early in the morning, he was soon ringing the bell at Hossein's house. When his bleary-eyed neighbour answered the door, Ali poured out the story of his dream. "Who was the figure in white?" he asked his neighbour. Hossein took down a book from a shelf, and surprised Ali by explaining that it was the Injil, or New Testament. Ali had always assumed the Injil was not true because Christians had corrupted its text, but when Hossein showed him the account of how Jesus was changed into a shining, white figure on the Mount of Transfiguration, he knew this was the person he had seen in his dream. Amazed, he took the book. Once he started to read it, he found he could not put it down.

In a matter of days, Ali had read the whole New Testament. He then started again from the beginning, and when he came to the account of the transfiguration of Jesus, the words of God from heaven to the three disciples hit him like a bolt of lightning: "This is my Son, the Beloved; with him I am well pleased; listen to him!" (Matt 17:5). From that moment on, Ali knew that the purpose of his life was to be a disciple of Jesus, listening to and obeying his truth, and sharing it with others. He prostrated himself on the floor in an act of submission, and the love of God washed over him, taking away the burden of his shame and lostness, and filling him with a glorious lightness. The only words he could find to describe this new reality was that he had been born again.

Ali ran to share his experience with Hossein, who heard his story with tears of joy and shouts of laughter. A fire was lit in their hearts, a burning desire to share this good news with as many people as possible. They started to pray and read the Bible together, and soon they were joined by some close friends. Of course, many scoffed, and some even cursed them for "selling their religion," accusing them of only changing their religion to make money.

In his enthusiasm, Ali told his father about his new faith. But his father, mortified that his eldest son had become an apostate, accused him of bringing shame and disgrace to the family name and threatened to cut him off from the family. When Ali stood his ground, his father got the local imam to come around to prove to him that Islam was the true, final, and perfect religion, much better than the corrupt Christianity of the West. Ali found it quite easy to refute the imam's arguments, and the confrontation only served to confirm him in his new faith. Finally, when Ali's uncles protested that this threat to the family reputation could not continue, his father convened a council of the extended family. Together, they solemnly declared that Ali was no longer one of theirs and decreed that no family member could talk to him or have any contact with him. This only increased Ali's determination to be a faithful follower of Jesus.

The little group of Christians began to grow. Through some missionaries in the capital, who heard about this group, Ali received a grounding in the Bible and training in ministry skills. The other members of the group recognized Ali's skills and respected his growing knowledge, which naturally led them to acknowledge him as their leader. New contacts were directed to this group by these missionaries, as well as through Christian websites and a satellite television channel. When a pastor from the capital visited them and laid hands on Ali in formal recognition of his position, Ali's spiritual authority increased. God blessed Ali's eagerness to serve, his unstinting hard work, and his passion for the gospel, and their numbers increased.

But as the numbers grew, some seemingly minor issues began to emerge. Ali found he had an ability to explain biblical truth in an illuminating and entertaining fashion, and he enjoyed it when everyone listened with rapt attention and, afterwards, came up to express their appreciation. When people praised him as their spiritual leader, Ali realized he was being given new honour and respect. As he grew into the role of an esteemed teacher, Ali's sermons gradually grew longer, fulfilling the cultural expectation that great teachers demonstrated their status with long speeches. When anyone questioned a point that he made, he felt it was an affront to his dignity, and gave them a cold shoulder, ignoring them for a couple of weeks to teach them a lesson.

After a while the missionaries in the capital heard about the growth of the new church, and provided funds to help them rent suitable premises and get a car to enable Ali to make evangelistic trips to outlying villages. These funds meant that Ali was able to help new believers who had money problems. These people then repaid their debt of gratitude, with loyalty to his leadership and willingness to help him with his projects. They became a core group in the church.

Not long after, there was an ugly incident with Abdullah. This young man had suddenly needed money for his mother's medical expenses, and Ali had been happy to help in the name of the church. But when Abdullah publicly questioned Ali's choice of worship leader, this "ingratitude" and challenge to

Ali's honour resulted in the young man being expelled from the group for his "rebellious spirit."

Muhammad, the worship leader whom Ali had appointed, turned out to be a talented musician with an ability to stir up a spirit of praise. People expressed their appreciation, and his reputation grew. Muhammed started to feel that Ali should listen to his opinions, but Ali felt threatened by this emerging leader. The tension between them grew until one day there was a sudden argument, which ended in a shouting match. Feeling dishonoured and shamed, Muhammad left the church, taking a group of friends with him. There were now two churches in the town, and although both continued to grow, because the leaders would not speak to each other there was mistrust and rivalry between the two groups.

From then on, things went downhill. Foreign money continued to roll in, and with it, invitations to Ali to speak at conferences in America, which in turn brought in more financial resources. He was able to get more done, and to help more people in his city, but the downside was the increasing jealousy among some of the older members. Hossein, who had been a founder member of the church along with Ali, began to question why Ali should enjoy all the prestige and perks, whereas he did not receive any recognition. Consumed by jealousy, he began to speculate that Ali was getting all these benefits because he was actually working for a foreign power. Despite knowing that there was no evidence for this, he began to whisper this story in the ears of others who were feeling left out, and soon there was a firestorm of gossip. Furious, Ali expelled his old friend from the group, which deeply saddened many church members as well as onlookers. Some people now thought that Ali's leadership was no different to that of the imam in the mosque that they had left not so long ago. They had come to the church because they had fallen in love with the grace of Jesus, and had thought that the church was a community founded on that same grace. As their disappointment grew, their faith withered, and gradually, they drifted away from the church. They still believed in Jesus, but they would never go back to church.

Ali was under tremendous pressure. To keep the church together, and to meet all the demands placed on him, he had to work harder and harder. His heart had been wounded by the conflicts and the loss of old friends, but now, he had no one with whom he could be open and admit his struggles. His reputation demanded that he keep up a perfect front. Behind the scenes, however, the emotional struggle was getting worse. Then he discovered that a glass or two of wine brought some relief. The occasional glass soon escalated into a habit that he could not control. Tragically, this spiralled into scandal and a fall from grace. Ali was compelled to leave town; and without their shepherd, the sheep soon scattered. A story that began with such bright promise ended in disaster – for Ali, for the church, and for the gospel.

First-Century Leadership

Although Ali's story is a composite fiction, the details are all drawn from incidents I have witnessed in the lives of leaders of new churches in the Muslim world. My calling is to see the kingdom of God established in Muslim hearts, but in forty years of ministry I have seen this tragic pattern repeated again and again: The Holy Spirit gloriously breaks into someone's life, and the truth of the word of God sets them free to follow and serve the Lord Jesus; their sincere zeal, deep devotion to Christ and their innate abilities secure early fruitfulness and establish them as church leaders, but the hierarchical and honour-driven models of leadership that are endemic to their cultures lead them to become dominant, controlling, and even abusive leaders; the Spirit is stifled and the fire is quenched, so that church becomes lifeless and monotonous for the members and a drudgery for the leaders. Time and time again promising breakthroughs for the gospel are undermined by faulty leadership, since leadership is the single most important factor for the success of any group.

For years I have been studying this problem, searching for a solution. As a Westerner, I was conscious of my own bias toward suspicion of all authority, an attitude that was nurtured by my years as a student protestor in the rebellious 60s. I did not want to impose my own cultural framework on Asian or African leaders, and I soon recognized that expecting them to exercise authority in the consultative style of democratic Westerners would be to condemn them to failure. Their followers would be confused by their seeming tentativeness and lose respect for them. I have a high view of Scripture, and believe that the Bible is God's truth, universally applicable for all nations. My search was for a biblical understanding that would correct faulty understandings of leadership in all cultures, addressing the weaknesses and blind spots of West as well as East.

A few years ago, I realized that Jesus and Paul lived in a very similar cultural setting to that of the Middle East today. Greco-Roman society in the first century was highly authoritarian, with Caesar demanding not just submission but even worship, and with fathers having the right to kill their own sons if they were disobedient. The pursuit of honour was the all-consuming goal that gave purpose to life. Anyone who has visited the ruins of an ancient Greek or Roman city will have seen the countless inscriptions chiselled into rock, honouring certain individuals and proclaiming their many achievements and titles for as long as the rock may last. This was the culture in which the apostles ministered, the culture from which their converts and new church leaders were drawn. How did they succeed in establishing Christian communities led by servant leaders when the very idea of a "servant leader" would have been a meaningless contradiction?

The heart of this book shows, from the New Testament, how first Jesus, and then his apostles, subverted the dominant cultural values in order to raise up leaders who could turn their backs on worldly authority and honour, and instead, give their lives to nurturing countercultural communities that were "turning the world upside down" (Acts 17:6). By embracing the disgrace of the cross, Jesus set an example that changed the world view of his disciples, making them willing to suffer the dishonour of being regarded as "the rubbish of the world" (1 Cor 4:13). Their remarkable achievement was to start a movement that, in time, succeeded in transforming the Roman Empire.

Give Up the Purple!

On 27 October 312, the successful Roman general Constantine led his army up to the River Tiber towards the gates of Rome. The next day, he would do battle with his rival, Maxentius, who stood between him and control of the Western half of the Empire. As Constantine was praying for divine help, he looked up to the sun and saw a cross shining in the sky with these words: "In this sign you will conquer." That night he had a vision, in which Christ explained the sign, and instructed him to use this sign of the cross as his banner against his enemies. The next day, Constantine won a sensational victory against an army twice the size of his own, and entered Rome as the triumphant conqueror.[2]

Within a year, Constantine issued an edict granting freedom of worship to Christians and ordering the return of all the churches confiscated during the terrible persecution of Diocletian a few years before. He decided to study Christianity for himself, and invited Bishop Lactantius to join his court in order to instruct him. After some time, he wrote to the Christians, making it clear that he owed his success to the Christian High God alone; thereafter, he progressively introduced legislation influenced by Christian ethics.

Just after Easter 337, twenty-five years after his vision of the cross, Constantine became seriously ill. Realizing that death was fast-approaching, he hurriedly arranged to go through the catechism – the teaching that all converts received before their baptism – and was finally baptized at Pentecost

---

2. This version of Constantine's vision is recounted by Eusebius, *Vit. Const.* 23.

of that year. It was a marvellous experience, in which he was "awestruck by the manifestation of divinely inspired power."[3] Constantine died soon afterwards.

Why did it take Constantine so long to decide to be baptized? The clue probably lies in the statement of repentance he made when he received the sacrament, in which he declared that from that time on he would give up wearing purple. He had known, since the beginning of his study of Christianity, that the catechism included the command to give up symbols of worldly pomp. The ultimate symbol of worldly power was the purple toga, worn only by the emperor and the cream of the aristocracy. Constantine could not bring himself to be baptized and submit to church teaching because he knew it would mean giving up this badge of honour. His world view had been shaped by life at court and in the army, so that for him the supreme good was found in *dignitas* – the pursuit of honour, wealth, a large retinue, showy costumes, titles, and formal address. The shame of giving up his purple toga would have been too much to endure.[4]

Purple dye was made from shellfish gathered off the coast of the eastern Mediterranean. Vast numbers of these tiny creatures were needed to manufacture sufficient quantities of dye, which made it inordinately expensive. Only the very rich could afford it. Consequently purple became a symbol of political power, and such an ostentatious display of affluence that the first-century writer Pliny the Elder described the craze for purple as "insanity."[5] Several early Roman emperors, worried about the effect of this statement on public morals, enacted legislation limiting its use. From the time of Nero, there was an imperial monopoly on purple dye and strict rules to ensure that only elite government officials could wear the prestigious purple toga.

Around a hundred years before Constantine, the church leader Hippolytus wrote, "If someone is a military governor, or the ruler of a city who wears the purple, he shall cease or he shall be rejected."[6] The early Christians expected new converts of rank to stop wearing purple or face exclusion from the church. Around the same time, Minucius Felix, a critic of the churches, scoffed, "They despise honours and purple robes."[7] Since the value system of the Roman Empire was founded on the pursuit of social status, the radically

---

3. Eusebius, *Vit. Const.* 4.62.

4. I am indebted to chapter 9 of Alan Kreider's book for this material about Constantine giving up the purple. Alan Kreider, *The Patient Ferment of the Early Church: The Improbable Rise of Christianity in the Roman Empire* (Grand Rapids: Baker, 2016).

5. Pliny, *Nat.* 9.127.

6. Hippolytus, *Trad. ap.* 16.9–10.

7. Minucius Felix, *Oct.* 8.

countercultural lifestyle of the believers was profoundly unsettling for the elite classes. The church had developed a discipleship process of catechism and baptism that succeeded in transforming the attitudes of converts from paganism. The experience of frequent worship and love feasts centred on the celebration of the Lord's Supper built communities of disciples committed to living out the example of Jesus and the apostles.

Unfortunately, these demands were a step too far for Constantine, whose sympathy for Christianity was not strong enough to make him willing to give up the symbols of his power and prestige. From his time on, church leaders began to wear gaudy robes of office and the architecture of new church buildings was based on the design of government buildings. Church and state became bedfellows, and the pristine glory of the vitality and purity of the early church gradually faded, with converts joining the church not to follow the way of Jesus, but, too often, with the hope of obtaining favours and advancement in the Empire. Leadership in the church became increasingly influenced by the Roman model of an authoritarian pursuit of honour, titles, and prestige. Yet, believers who would be leaders in the church today are still called on to "give up the purple"!

2

Patron Leadership

Why Do Churches Fail?

In the late 1980s my wife and I were helping to plant a church in Ankara, Turkey. Progress was painfully slow. After more than twenty years of Protestant missionary effort in the city our little group only numbered twenty or so members, many of whom were struggling in their new faith.

Then we began to receive wonderful reports, coming over the border from Bulgaria, of a remarkable outpouring of the Holy Spirit among the Millet people, Turkish-speaking Roma who had become Muslims during the time of the Ottoman Empire. There were credible accounts of people being healed, even being raised from the dead. Enthusiastic worshippers were crowding into new churches, and by 1995 leaders estimated there were ten thousand converts in the new churches. Yet, just twelve years later, a church census recorded just six thousand members. What had gone wrong?

Studies of church planting usually focus on the success stories, seeking to identify the factors that may explain a movement of extraordinary growth. Sometimes it can be just as useful to examine our failures, by looking at instances of church decline. Australian missiologists Richard and Evelyn Hibbert had worked in Bulgaria during the heady days of the 1990s, and went back there to do their doctoral research into why people had left the churches.[1] Rather than ask pastors why people had defected from their churches, they asked the defectors themselves. Three clear patterns emerged:

1. All but one of the people they talked to said they still believed in Jesus, even though they no longer went to church. They were

---

1. Richard Y. Hibbert, "Why Do They Leave?: An Ethnographic Investigation of Defection from Turkish-Speaking Roma Churches in Bulgaria," *Missiology* 41 (2013): 315.

defectors from the church, not apostates from the faith. The one exception to this was a woman who had gone back to Islam because she had married an imam!

2.   Many complained that they did not feel accepted by others in the churches, often because they found it difficult to live a Christian lifestyle. They felt ashamed and were afraid of being rejected and gossiped about.

3.   More than half of those interviewed complained about the over-bearing manner of the pastors, who had adopted the authoritarian leadership style found in Bulgarian society, politics and churches. Some specific problems mentioned were:
    - A dictatorial leadership style. Pastors became more controlling, even forbidding people to visit others without their permission.
    - Failure to show care or warmth. Pastors became aloof and remote, and did not visit or support members when they were struggling.
    - Unilateral decision-making by pastors.
    - Condemning attitudes. Pastors would shame members whom they disapproved of by publicly condemning them from the pulpit, sometimes even repeating things they had been told in confidence.
    - Competitive spirit between pastors. Church members grew disillusioned when their pastor criticized other pastors and appeared to find satisfaction in pointing out their failings. It seemed pastors were more interested in boosting the reputation of their church – and themselves – than in seeing the advance of the kingdom of God in their town.

A similar scenario played out among the Muslim Uyghurs living in the east of Kazakhstan along the Chinese border. The economic chaos and ideological vacuum caused by the collapse of communism in 1990 resulted in a season of rapid church growth across central Asia. In a particular town, in 1996, there were a hundred believers, a pastor, and a building where the congregation gathered. By 2010 that church had completely disappeared. Phillip,[2] a veteran missionary, interviewed many of these lapsed church members. His findings were strikingly similar to those in the Bulgarian case study:

---

2. Not his real name. He shared these findings with me in personal correspondence.

1. Everyone still affirmed their faith in Christ. A lady who had not been to church for fourteen years proudly reported that she had declared to some Jehovah's Witnesses, "We are Christians and will remain so until the end!"

2. People did not feel safe or accepted, so that attending church services became too uncomfortable. Phillip explained, "It was mostly gossip, people taking offence, holding grudges, being unable to humble themselves to ask forgiveness and pursue reconciliation."

3. A common complaint was poor leadership. "Many were mad at the pastor over what they considered a whole string of insensitive remarks." He blamed others for the failure of the church rather than taking responsibility himself.

In both instances of church decline we see the same two key factors: poor community formation and poor leadership. Of these, poor leadership is the more fundamental problem because we know that the culture and ethos of any group is set by the example and the teaching of its leadership. What causes well-meaning pastors to fail their flocks so consistently and so badly? The reason lies in their understanding of leadership, shaped by the patron-client model that is common in hierarchical cultures.

Patron Leaders

What is the position of fathers in your culture? Some Iranian and Arab friends have told me that when their father entered the room, they were expected to stand up, not lounge back in their chairs, and certainly never smoke in his presence. Showing respect to their father was a cardinal principle of life – and this included studying his favoured subject at university and only marrying someone he approved of, perhaps even someone he chose. The benefit of relating to their father in this way was that when they did get married, the family ensured that the couple's new home was fully furnished with the most modern appliances and the most stylish furniture.

Having lived in Asia for nearly twenty years, I am taken aback when I hear children in the West address their parents by their first names. Once these children reach their teens, parents seem to have little control over their lives – they will give advice about university and marriage partners, but certainly cannot dictate. Since young people tend to marry later in life, by this time they have already worked for some years and are able to contribute far more towards the cost of their wedding. Although parents are happy to help with the costs of setting up a new home, they don't consider themselves responsible for providing the latest or most fashionable furniture or fittings.

Authority is a fundamental element of any social structure. From an early age, our understanding of authority is shaped by our fathers. We observe how our fathers relate to our mothers and siblings; we are also deeply influenced by the way our elder brothers and sisters treat us. Unlike in the highly individualistic West – where I am more likely to do what I want, to resent people who violate my autonomy by telling me what to do, and to care little what others think of me – in Asia and Africa people identify themselves far more closely with their families and larger social units. Since being part of the family is so important, respecting and obeying authority within the family is crucial. By the same token, the family feels a strong sense of obligation to look after the needs of the members, and feels a shared shame if it is unable to do so. The honour of the family is at stake, and their standing in the community is of vital importance.

As a result, the prevailing model of leadership in the Global South and East is patron-client. The word "patron" is taken from the Latin *pater* (father), and patrons are authority figures who care for their clients in a variety of ways – providing financial assistance, introductions to influential people, or spiritual advice. Clients reciprocate by giving respect in the form of loyalty, obedience, and praise. In this reciprocal relationship patrons gain what is most important to them – honour – and clients gain security in knowing that someone is looking after them in an insecure world. Fathers are the archetypal patrons, but patron-client relationships are found throughout society since all authority figures tend to be viewed in this way. Teachers, employers, and political leaders all command this kind of respect, and are expected to care for their subordinates.

I will argue that the patron-client model is not in itself wrong, and can be a healthy, mutually satisfying relationship. Unfortunately, given our fallen nature, it is not surprising that it often becomes corrupt and abusive. Here are twelve symptoms of toxic patron leadership:

1. Patron leaders use their authority in a domineering and controlling way. Patron leaders think that because they have helped their followers they have purchased their loyalty – and so they expect obedience in every detail of their lives. Disgruntled and alienated church members in Bulgaria complained that their pastors even tried to dictate whom they could and could not socialize with. It is possible that some of these pastors were thinking of Paul's instructions on church discipline in 1 Corinthians 5. But Paul was addressing instances of

serious sin – such as sexual immorality between a man and his stepmother – or a settled lifestyle of sin among those who claimed to be Christians. He was certainly not referring to "the immoral of this world" (1 Cor 5:10). If pastors order members not to socialize with others in order to enforce their own authority and maintain a sense of control, they have both confused and abused the God-given authority which is intended to uphold holiness among the saints.

2. Patron leaders expect to be consulted about minor matters.
Patron leaders are offended when they are not consulted or kept informed about everything, and perceive such failures as slights. For instance, some church members were greeted coldly by the pastor because they had gone on a trip to the capital without letting him know beforehand.

3. Patron leaders are poor at delegation.
Patron leaders struggle to share authority because it is so key to their self-respect. Even when they do ask someone to take charge of a particular activity, they may interfere or intervene and take over without any consultation or discussion. Once, I had been asked to run an outreach program. I arrived at the usual time only to find that my leader had already gathered the team and was addressing them, without having given me any warning or explanation. He assumed that since the whole church was under his authority he did not need to inform me beforehand. I felt angry and humiliated! This kind of behaviour stifles the development of new leaders and undermines their confidence.

4. Patron leaders silence the truth by suppressing criticism.
Anyone who questions their decisions or criticizes their ministry is seen as a threat to the patron leader's standing. When a gifted and zealous young person makes suggestions about how things may be done better, this is seen as implicit criticism of the way the pastor has been doing things. Patron pastors view such suggestions as an attack on their honour and so, instead of discussing the issues and being open to new ideas, they take offence and express their displeasure – perhaps even by removing the young person from some ministry in order to "take them down a peg or two."

Once members realize that they are expected not to question the pastor's wisdom, it is difficult for them to draw attention to awkward facts. Even if everyone knows the pastor's plan is not working, no one can openly say so. As a result, a polite fiction takes the place of unpalatable truth. There may be outward harmony for some time, but sooner or later unpleasant realities are exposed.

5.   Patron leaders discipline by shunning and exclusion.

People frequently discover they have offended the pastor only when they arrive at church and find that their greeting is not returned. They are being shunned, without any explanation, in order to bring them into line. In collective cultures the harmony of the group is more important than it is in individualistic ones, so people are better at reading between the lines and understanding the unspoken message. But Jesus exhorts us, "If another member of the church sins against you, go and point out the fault when the two of you are alone. If the member listens to you, you have regained that one" (Matt 18:15). By failing to do this, the pastor is missing a great opportunity for discipleship.

Church discipline is difficult and uncomfortable. Although it is a biblical requirement it is often carried out in such a harsh and heavy-handed manner that it creates more problems than it solves. Being accepted as a member of the group is more important in collective cultures, and so everyone is concerned about who is "in" and who is "out." The appropriate exercise of church discipline may get confused with social control, and legalism on the basis of rules may replace grace for new believers who are struggling to be set free of their past habits. In the Bulgarian case study we saw that this was a significant reason why believers left the church.

6.   Patrons compete with and criticize other leaders and other churches.

Since patron pastors derive honour and reputation from their position in the church, the bigger the church, the greater their status. Therefore, another pastor with a bigger church is viewed as a rival. Patron pastors may deal with their irritation and envy by making comments to put down the second pastor, or by sharing juicy bits of gossip: "Of course we praise the Lord for our brother's ministry. But do you know *why* all these people are going to his church? Actually, it is because . . ."

7.   Patrons view emerging leaders as a threat.

King Saul was threatened by the young David's popularity, which stemmed from his victories in battle. Similarly, established pastors may feel threatened by younger leaders with new ideas and growing reputations. One of the core responsibilities of leaders is to raise up new leaders for the next generation, but this is difficult when their own identity is derived from the honour of their current role. The result is that promising young leaders are deliberately hindered from achieving too much prominence and success; they in turn may grow frustrated and break away – perhaps with a group of their peers – to start another church.

While praising God for the large numbers of Iranians, around the world, who are coming to faith in Christ, we must acknowledge that Iranian churches are also characterized by their disunity and splits. Oksnevad's study into disharmony in Iranian churches revealed that although Iranians have great respect and affection for their leaders, when disappointed or frustrated by their pastor-patrons their devotion turns to enmity, and they start rival churches out of spite.[3]

Dr Arley Loewen recounts a Persian story of a great wrestler who had a promising student. One day the student decided he had learned all there was to learn from his master and challenged him to a contest in the presence of the Shah. The two were indeed evenly matched and the bout looked like it would never end, until the master pulled a trick he had never shown his student. "You never taught me that one!" protested the student. "Did you really think I would teach you every move I know, and allow you to surpass me?' retorted the master.[4]

8.   Patrons cannot admit to weaknesses.

Since honour depends on their position, patron pastors can never admit to ignorance or weakness for fear of losing their authority. One pastor admitted that when asked a question he could not answer he would bluff: "I can't let them think there is something I do not know, or else they will no longer respect me as their teacher." Pretending omniscience is a dangerous path! The deeper problem with this is that it becomes very difficult for patron leaders to share their struggles and get needed support from trusted peers.

9.   Patrons avoid transparency and accountability.

Questioning feels like a challenge, and enquiries feel like threats, so transparency and accountability are avoided. A missionary organization had given funds to a church in the Middle East. A few years later, I was sent to find out from the church leaders how the funds entrusted to them had been used. From the irritation evident in the manner and tone of their responses, I realized that my questions had made them feel that we doubted their integrity, and they found this shameful.

---

3. Roy Oksnevad, "BMB Discipleship: An Investigation into the Factors Leading to Disharmony within the Iranian Churches in the Diaspora," *St Francis Magazine* 8, no. 4 (2012): 397–434.

4. Arley Loewen, *New Horizons for Afghanistan: Principles of Leadership Development* (Kabul: Faisal Publications, 2008).

10. Patrons cling to leadership roles.

Church leaders who derive their identity and status from their position find it extremely difficult to pass on the baton to someone else. Somehow, no one else seems quite good enough, so they just keep soldiering on! The result is older and older leaders who are less and less able to innovate or to see their blind spots.

Quite often the only person considered trustworthy enough to take on the ministry is their own son, and so leadership becomes an inheritance. Since their son is one with them, his taking on the leadership is viewed as an extension of their honour and not a threat. Although it is quite appropriate to pass on a business or land to an heir – because that is personal property that the owner can rightfully bequeath – leadership in God's church is a gift of God, not ours to give to whomever we wish. Again, the fundamental mistake is confusing *God's* kingdom and authority with *my* kingdom and authority.

11. Patrons seek to accumulate perks of office.

Status symbols of leadership demonstrate the honour and glory associated with the role. It is expected that the leader will have a bigger house, a bigger office, a bigger car, and more foreign travel than anyone else. Some reward for hard work and responsibility is appropriate, but these perks can become an end in themselves, driving a lifestyle that contradicts the message being preached. Add a lack of accountability to the mix and the stage is set for dishonest self-enrichment, ultimately leading to a fall and resulting in the loss of spiritual authority.

The sense of entitlement to "special treats" opens the way to spiritual, emotional and sexual abuse. The greater the pastor's authority, the more members feel obliged to submit, which may lead to inappropriate intimacy. Of course, this danger is not limited to the Global South, since the tendency of power to corrupt is found in every society and culture. The Roman Catholic Church has been shaken to its core by a string of sexual abuse scandals – not surprising, given its opaque structure and the privileged position of its priests. As we consider the scandals affecting megachurch pastors around the world, we realize that we Protestants are not much better.

12. Patrons burn out on conflict and emotional pressures.

These pastors have placed themselves in an almost impossible position, and many burn out. The way they perceive their office and conduct their duties almost inevitably leads to conflict with others. The need to keep up appearances keeps them isolated from anyone who might come alongside to help, and this adds emotional pressure. They are inspired by true devotion and work incredibly hard to keep the ministry going, but the price is very high. Their families – who usually suffer the most from the consequences of their driven lifestyles – are often unable to become necessary havens for rest and renewal. It is too much for many people and only a few can sustain the effort. Tragically, so many pastors, who started out with high hopes and sincere aspirations, end up defeated and disappointed. It is even more tragic for those followers who put their trust in them, only to walk away disillusioned by the whole religious charade, concluding, "It is no different from the mosque!"

Healthy Patronage

Just because many patrons become controlling and dominant, it does not mean this is always the case. The patron-client model is not wrong in itself, and can provide the framework for healthy, caring, and productive relationships. Claudia, a Brazilian missionary in Bosnia, has warm memories of her father's example as a church elder. Although the family were not well off, he would raid the scant supplies in their larder to feed poor young believers who came to him for help. The family were upset, but the young men were deeply grateful and came back to spend time with the father, taking the opportunity to study the Bible together. Like his missionary daughter, Claudia, they also took on his values and mission for themselves, committed to the gospel and became pillars in the church. He became their patron when he gave to them unselfishly, not to boost his status but out of genuine concern. His patronage was far more than food, as he taught Scripture and modelled Christian values. The young men's respect for him was not at all self-serving, but sincere and self-giving; and they were committed to help him further the cause he cared about.

A relationship like this, founded on genuine concern and sincere loyalty, has enormous potential for transformational discipleship. Values and character are transferred from heart to heart, so the deeper the heart-linking and the more open each is to the other, the greater the imprint of one heart on the other. The disciple submits to the master, and the more complete that submission the greater the degree to which the disciple will imitate the master. The word "submission" sounds dangerous to Western ears, because we have become very suspicious of authority, but I would argue that it is biblical. Elisha "used to pour water on the hands of Elijah" (2 Kgs 3:11), which means he was his personal servant; and when Elijah was taken up to heaven Elisha inherited a double portion of his spirit. Inheriting a double portion was the privilege of the eldest son, and Elisha demonstrated his sonship by continuing the mission of his spiritual father, striving to eradicate Baal worship in Israel. Timothy was

Paul's "true" or "sincere" child (1 Tim 1:2), and his submission to Paul went so far as to allow Paul to have him circumcised!

Patron-client relationships used to be common in the West too, but we have now forgotten how to handle the subtle nuances. We value our autonomy so much that we resist the deep intimacy, loss of privacy, and personal surrender that submission implies. We feel awkward when we are honoured, and well-meaning praise makes us cringe because it sounds like flattery. We feel embarrassed when someone tries to serve us. As a result, when we become missionaries, teachers, business people or NGO directors in countries with more collective cultures, our relationships with those around us often end in the mutual disappointment of mismatched expectations. Because of our passports, and the resources we usually command, we are inevitably seen as patrons, but we do not understand the privileges and responsibilities that the role carries. The nice words of respect sound insincere; the requests for help feel like manipulative imposition; it seems as if everyone is trying to exploit us and we become weary and cynical. Of course, our national friends and colleagues suffer similar disappointments as they misread our signals and have expectations of us that cannot be fulfilled. It is also true that – because we are not familiar with the rules of patron-client relationships – we do allow ourselves to be manipulated and exploited by unscrupulous characters. As outsiders in that culture, we are unable to discern people's motives as accurately as insiders, and so we are perceived as naive and gullible.

Del Chinchen, reflecting on his African experience, suggested some guidelines to help us Westerners navigate these relationships. He pictures the ideal patron-client relationship as starting with a small gift of appreciation from the prospective client – as a sign of admiration and a signal that the client would like to enter into a relationship with and learn from this patron. The prospective patron responds with a visit or a request for a small task to be performed. The two develop the relationship through incremental steps which build trust, so that a small favour given meets with a response of a cheerful act of service. The mutual trust and commitment grow stronger until patrons feels confident to help in large and significant ways, and clients know they can give themselves to their patron's agenda without fear of being abused.[5]

Chinchen constructed this table to contrast what he terms "Corrupt Patronage" and "Redeemed Patronage":[6]

---

5. Delbert Chinchen, "The Patron-Client System: A Model of Indigenous Leadership," *Evangelical Missions Quarterly* 31, no. 4 (1995): 446–451.

6. Chinchen, "Patron-Client System."

Corrupt Patronage	Redeemed Patronage
Starts with client making a large demand	Starts with client making a small gift of appreciation
False hopes, false securities, intentional creation of fictitious insecurities	Truth, honesty, openness, integrity, promises fulfilled
Weak, self-serving relationships	Strong, authentic relationships
Utilitarian and materialistic	Genuine and sincere
Proud patron insists on titles and status	Humble patron honours the client
Proud and unwilling to visit the client	Visits and nurtures the client
Proud patron, above questioning	Humble patron, who can admit faults
Insists on balanced reciprocity	Unconditional, self-sacrificing love
Possessive, keeps client inferior	Aims for client's maturity and independence

As far back as the first century AD, the Roman philosopher Seneca compared an ideal patron-client relationship to a dance of three graces: the grace of generous giving on the part of the patron, the grace of receiving on the part of the client, and then the grace of the client's grateful response. As the graceful dancers turn in their circle the benefit given comes back to the benefactor, and the dance becomes a joyful web of mutual relationships. The intricate footwork demands sensitivity and skill. Meanness or ingratitude disrupt the harmony. But when the dance is done well it becomes something profoundly beautiful. The relationship between a caring patron and a loyal client can become a transformational interaction for the glory of God.

3

Paul in Corinth[1]

Paul and the Corinthians

Paul stood on the beach at Troas, his eyes scanning the horizon for a sail. It was the autumn of AD 55 and he shivered in the chilly wind. Where was Titus? Paul knew he should be getting ready for the evening's meeting with the new believers, some of whom were showing great potential, but he was desperate for news from Corinth. He had sent Titus there to sort out the mess after his last disastrous visit, and was expecting him on the next boat.

Paul's heart was a storm of conflicting emotions. On the one hand, he felt a deep and intense affection for the believers in Corinth, like that of a father for his children. He cherished fond memories of those early days of his first visit, and the heady excitement of glorious victories in the midst of great conflict. Soon after his arrival, the Jewish leaders had abused him and kicked him out of the synagogue, and then fabricated a case against him before the new Roman consul Gallio.[2] For a while, he had thought he might be in for another beating with the Roman rods, but Gallio was smart enough to see through their ploy. Despite this opposition, Crispus from the synagogue had believed in Jesus as Messiah, and another synagogue official Sosthenes was beaten up for having accepted Jesus as Messiah. Dear Gaius and Stephanas had opened their homes to host a couple of the new house churches. Paul smiled as he remembered some of the disreputable ragamuffins whose lives had been turned around – idolaters, thieves, drunkards, promiscuous philanderers,

---

1. For much of the material in this chapter I am indebted to the following: Paul W. Barnett, *The Corinthian Question* (Nottingham: Apollos, 2011); David E. Garland, *2 Corinthians*, NAC 29 (Nashville: B&H, 1999); Murray J. Harris, *The Second Epistle to the Corinthians*, NIGTC (Grand Rapids: Eerdmans, 2005).
2. Acts 18:1–17.

homosexuals, gluttons! What incredible times of worship they had experienced as they tasted the joy of the Holy Spirit and the wonder at his gifts! He felt an intense longing to see them all again. The deep heart-linking he felt with them was well worth the trials and suffering.

Then it had all gone sour. It started when Paul was in Ephesus and Chloe's folks sent a report of disunity (1 Cor 1:11), and the list of problems got longer and longer. The believers from a wealthy elite background were continuing to behave in just the same old way – suing one another in the law courts, eating sacrificial meat with their old friends at feasts in the temples, and gorging themselves in front of their poor, hungry brethren at the church love feasts just like they used to at their old banquets.

Paul wrote a letter – which we know as 1 Corinthians – and later went over to Corinth in person, for a visit that turned out to be so painful that he still winced at the memory (2 Cor 2:1). There was one individual flagrantly sleeping with his stepmother, and the church refused to do anything about it. On the contrary, they were proud of their freedom from outmoded taboos! When Paul demanded action they opposed him to his face, telling him he was not good enough to be their apostle. They wanted a smooth-talking, flashy, sophisticated figure who would fit in with their idea of what a leader should be. Paul's rhetoric was weak, his appearance shabby, and he demeaned himself in their eyes by working with his hands in his tent-making business (2 Cor 10:10). They publicly insulted him and he had no other choice but to leave battered and bruised.

The only thing Paul could do was to write another letter, stained with his tears, and send it to the Corinthians through Titus (2 Cor 2:4). Now he was in Troas, waiting for Titus to return with news of how they had responded to his pleas. As he looked out for a ship coming from Corinth, he prayed again for God's grace to turn the situation around. Glimpsing a sail, he ran to the dock. One by one the passengers got off, but there was no Titus! Paul asked when the next ship would arrive, and was told that this was the last one before the winter storms made sailing in the Mediterranean too dangerous. His heart sank, because he knew he would have to leave Troas and take the land route through Macedonia to Corinth. He was so concerned about the dear saints in Corinth that he could hardly focus on the ministry in Troas. The anxiety for their well-being gnawing in the pit of his stomach was worse than any beating or shipwreck (2 Cor 11:28)!

Paul Confronts Social Values

Taking the land route to Corinth had the advantage of giving Paul plenty of time to think about the issues he was facing. He knew the opposition against him was driven mainly by the social elite who had come into the church, but whose values had not been changed by the gospel. Their motivation was still the pursuit of honour and the accumulation of titles. In the highly-stratified Greco-Roman society, they were most concerned about their reputation – which depended on coming from a good family, enjoying great wealth, and being praised by others for being generous and brave. They saw life as a competition to improve their social standing, and everything they did was calculated to further that end, whether it was inviting key allies to add lustre to their feasts or shaming opponents in the law courts. They wanted speeches made in their honour and inscriptions to permanently record their glory. As the upper class, they wielded great power, with authority to order everyone else around, to humiliate them, and in the case of their slaves, to order their flogging and even crucifixion.

For these people, Paul's manner and lifestyle was a major stumbling block. For a start, they thought his speech was contemptible, quite unlike that of the skilled and eloquent rhetorician Apollos (Acts 18:24). For people in the first century, rhetoric was one of the most important skills because it was vital for the pursuit of honour in public debates, the law courts and at social events. In fact, higher education consisted mostly of training in public speaking, and it was fashionable to use flowery language and complicated sentences. Paul's letters show that while he certainly had mastery of language, he was not going to show off or play these rhetorical games.

In addition, Paul's physical appearance was weak, and failed to cut the impressive figure people expected of a leader. The Romans looked up to strong leaders whose powerful physique reflected their dominant personalities. A contemporary example would be President Putin's photos of his well-honed torso and rippling biceps, which he knows will reassure the Russians that they have the kind of leader they want.

The Corinthians were particularly distressed by Paul's strange insistence on working with his hands, like some lower-class artisan. In Corinth, no one who aspired to be a gentleman would be caught engaged in physical labour – that was what slaves were for. Even worse was Paul's reason for continuing his work of tent-making – to avoid having to accept their financial help. In the ancient world, wealthy patrons were accustomed to supporting itinerant philosophers as their clients. In return, the philosophers were happy to eulogize their patrons, and the patrons also gained honour when these clever philosophers dazzled guests at their feasts. Paul realized that becoming part of such a system would compromise his freedom to speak out and challenge the values on which it was based. He was willing to accept help from the church at Philippi *after* he had left them, since that made them partners in his mission; but he would not accept help from the Corinthians while he was still in Corinth, since that would blunt the sharp edge of his message.

As for the elite in the Corinthian church, they considered Paul a weak fool, someone to be laughed at, like a buffoon in the comedies by writers like Plautus. These plays were usually about slaves, pathetic wretches in ridiculously ill-fitting clothes, so funny when they were beaten and driven out of their homes. The biggest laugh would come at the end, when they endured the ultimate humiliation of crucifixion.[3] Paul was well aware that this was how he appeared to his opponents.

Somewhere along the road through Macedonia Paul finally met up with Titus, who eagerly recounted the incredible influence of Paul's tear-stained letter on the believers in Corinth. They now felt great sorrow for what they had done to Paul. They repented of their attitudes and actions, and were eager to do whatever was necessary to restore the relationship, including punishing the individual who had caused such grievous offence (2 Cor 7:11). Paul was overcome by joy as his hopes were fulfilled and he realized that his confidence in them had not been misplaced. After so many days of dread, what wonderful relief. Hallelujah!

There was, however, one group still standing out against Paul – the "super apostles" who disputed Paul's personal authority. They too were Jews, probably claiming to represent the real apostles in Jerusalem. Their version of the gospel, however, was fatally flawed, glossing over the offence of the cross, and preaching an experience of the Holy Spirit that emphasized ecstatic experiences but ignored the supreme imperative of love. Paul felt jealous and angry: jealous because these "super apostles" were seducing the believers he loved; angry because his good work in the lives of the believers was being undone. He sat down and wrote another letter – our 2 Corinthians – and sent it on ahead with Titus and some other brothers, in order to prepare for his imminent arrival.

This letter instructs the Corinthians to restore the brother they had punished. Now that he is assured of their cooperation, Paul also gives instructions about the large gift he is planning to take for the poor believers

---

3. Laurence Welborn, "Paul's Appropriation of the Role of the Fool in 1 Corinthians 1–4," *Biblical Interpretation* 10, no. 4 (2002): 420–435.

in Jerusalem. Then, in the final chapters, he deals with the "super apostles," determined to destroy the strongholds of their poisonous arguments. He does this by launching into an extraordinary "boast." Boasting was a normal practice for leaders in the first century, as it was an obvious way to push themselves forward. As a good Jew, and shaped by the Old Testament view of God, Paul was loath to boast, but since it was the only language his opponents understood, he realized that he would also have to boast. His boast, however (2 Cor 11:16–12:10), undermines the very basis of their boasting and reasserts the true nature of apostolic authority.

Paul begins by pointing out that he too is Jewish, but then goes on to list all his sufferings. Lists of sufferings and hardships were a common way for leaders to assert their right to great rank and honour. Alexander the Great – the archetypal great man of the classical era, known for his desire to be the most famous man in the whole world – used to enumerate his wounds and scars, along with accounts of the glorious battles in which they were inflicted. Paul's list is different in that he remembers countless floggings, five whippings from the Jews, three beatings with rods from the Romans, and a stoning. Paul's back must have been a mass of scar tissue. These are not the honourable wounds on the front of a soldier going into battle, but disgraceful marks of humiliation on the back of a slave who has been punished.[4] The Roman writer Apuleius described a group of slaves he met: "Their skin was everywhere embroidered with purple welts from their many beatings. Their backs, scarred from floggings, were covered by torn, patchwork garments."[5] Paul deliberately boasts of this shame.

Similarly, Paul tells a little joke against himself, about how he was let down the wall of Damascus in a basket. The Roman army had a well-known award for valour, the *corona moralis* or "crown of the wall," given to the first soldier who got to the top of the wall of the city they were besieging, in the face of all the missiles being thrown down at him. Paul does not boast of his heroic exploits going up the wall, but the comic sight of his undignified escape coming down in a basket![6]

The "super apostles" would be the kind of people who would delight to boast about their amazing supernatural adventures as a way of authenticating their ministries. They would recount their astonishing visions and retell

---

4. Jennifer A. Glancy, "Boasting of Beatings (2 Corinthians 11:23–25)," *Journal of Biblical Literature* 123, no. 1 (Spring 2004): 99–135.

5. Apuleius, *Metam.* 9.12.

6. E. A. Judge, "The Conflict of Educational Aims in New Testament Thought," *International Journal of Christianity & Education* 9 (1966): 32–45.

in detail their extraordinary miracles. Paul, therefore, has to talk about his spiritual experiences. There is no doubt that Paul had a rich interior life, but he is strangely reluctant to talk about it, preferring to speak in the third person about "a person in Christ" (2 Cor 12:2). Having established that he has had a vision of heaven, he refuses to titillate with any further details. Although the "super apostles" would boast about many healings, Paul limits himself to his own personal affliction from Satan, and his unsuccessful threefold prayer for deliverance. We know there were many other instances of healing in Paul's career, but now he emphasizes that this apostle could not even see his own illness healed! The point of it all is the Lord's words, "My grace is sufficient for you, for power is made perfect in weakness" (2 Cor 12:9).

This glorying in weakness and shame does not mean Paul lacked spiritual authority. Indeed, by the end of the letter, the tone is forceful, as Paul says he is coming as a judge to take evidence from witnesses, endowed with the authority to build up or tear down, warning them that if necessary he can act harshly (2 Cor 13:1–10). Being a servant leader does not mean being diffident or lacking in drive and direction.

The letter achieved what Paul hoped for, and he was able to spend the winter of AD 56 in Corinth. From there, he wrote his letter to the Roman Christians, in which he happily reported that the saints in "Macedonia and Achaia have been pleased to share their resources with the poor among the saints at Jerusalem" (Rom 15:26). The church in Corinth had swung around behind Paul, acknowledging his apostolic authority and enthusiastically contributing to his project of sending a gift to the mother church in Jerusalem.

This was an astonishing victory. If Paul had defended his authority and defeated the "super apostles" by out-boasting them – deploying his greater learning, keener intellect, and more spectacular miracles – then he would have won the battle but lost the war. The deeper issue was to subvert the culture and values that formed the basis of the appeal made by the "super apostles." If he had countered them on their own terms, fighting the battle on their home ground, he may have established his superiority, but the world view ruling the church would have remained in place. The only way to "tear down the stronghold" (2 Cor 10:4) of the culture of honour and power was to use the weapons of his shame and weakness. This was a high-risk strategy, but Paul believed that since Jesus himself "was crucified in weakness, but lives by the power of God" (2 Cor 13:4), he too would be vindicated and given true spiritual authority in the eyes of the church.

Leaders of new churches that are located in profoundly non-Christian cultures must understand that they will only see these cultures transformed by living countercultural lives. This will mean following Paul down the narrow path of suffering, bearing shame and disgrace, drawing ever nearer to the cross. In difficult times, they will have to resist the temptation to revert to the default culture of their upbringing. Their reward will be in seeing true transformation of lives and communities.

4

Paul in Philippi

Paul's Understanding of the Cross

Life in Philippi

Around AD 50, five years or so before his struggle with the church in Corinth, Paul was in Troas, trying to discern where he should go for the next phase of his missionary adventure. One night he had a powerful vision, in which he saw a man from Macedonia cry, "Come over to Macedonia and help us" (Acts 16:9). Straight away he and his companions found a boat sailing to Philippi, the chief city of Macedonia, and plunged into a culturally different world.

Philippi was more Roman than any other city Paul had lived in. It had been established as a Roman colony in 42 BC when Octavian – later to become the emperor Augustus – revenged himself on Brutus and Cassius, the assassins of Julius Caesar, by defeating them in a great battle just outside the town. Octavian then faced the problem of what to do with his troops, since taking so many unemployed soldiers back to Rome would be a recipe for disaster. His solution was to give the town and the surrounding lands to his veterans. The unfortunate native inhabitants were suddenly dispossessed of their property and dropped to the bottom of the social pecking order, making way for their new Roman masters!

Philippi was very Roman. With a large segment of the population descended from Augustus's veterans there was an intense loyalty to Rome and to Roman culture. Throughout the Empire as a whole around 14 percent of the population held Roman citizenship, but archaeological evidence suggests that 40 percent of the people in Philippi were citizens.[1] The profusion of inscriptions

---

1. Much of the material in this chapter is based on a book by Biola New Testament professor Joseph H. Hellerman, *Embracing Shared Ministry: Power and Status in the Early Church and Why It Matters Today* (Grand Rapids: Kregel, 2013).

chiselled into stone monuments all over the town are mute evidence of how they saw themselves. They were all keenly aware of their social status, and how they were doing in the *cursus honorum*, the race for honour. They would have heartily agreed with the Roman writer Cicero when he said, "By nature we yearn and hunger for honour, and once we have glimpsed some part of its radiance there is nothing we are not prepared to bear and suffer in order to secure it."[2] Honour was expressed in titles of public office they acquired, and so a typical inscription would read:

> Publius Marius Valens, son of Publius, from the tribe Voltinia, honored with the decorations of Decurion, aedile, also Decurion of Philippi, priest of the divine Antoninus Pius, duumvir, sponsor of games.[3]

Publius starts with the honour that springs from who he is, with his family background and citizenship, and then moves on to the achievements and honours he has gained. Around 50 percent of the inscriptions in Philippi mention the tribe of Voltinia,[4] one of the tribes all Roman citizens were assigned to, and the point of the reference is to make clear that Publius was a citizen. The *decurions* were a third level of the elite classes, under senators and equestrians; the *aedile* were in charge of public works and games; the *duumvir* (two men) were leading magistrates who held power in the city. Publius also wants everyone to know that he sponsored the games once, which he would have done out of his own pocket in a show of generosity in order to boost his status. Running in the race for honour was not a cheap option, but for the Romans honour was more important than wealth, and wealth was just a means of gaining honour.

Paul and Silas's arrival in Philippi

Paul, Silas and Luke disembarked from their ship and set about looking for the opportunities they believed the Lord had prepared for them to proclaim the gospel. Usually, they would have gone to the Jewish synagogue; but since there was no synagogue, they found a prayer group down by the river. The group

---

2. Cicero, *Tusc.* 2.24.58.

3. Joseph H. Hellerman, *Reconstructing Honor in Roman Philippi: Carmen Christi as Cursus Pudorum*, Society for New Testament Studies Monograph Series 132 (Cambridge: Cambridge University Press), 97.

4. Peter Pilhofer, *Philippi, Band 1: Die erste christliche Gemeinde Europas*, WUNT (Tübingen: Mohr Sieback, 1995).

was led by Lydia, a seller of luxury goods, a dealer in purple cloth. God opened Lydia's heart to the message, and she persuaded Paul to accept her patronage by staying with her household. As Paul moved around town he attracted the attention of a slave girl who was possessed by a spirit of fortune telling and was making a lot of money for her owners. The girl started following Paul around, shouting, "These men are slaves of the Most High God, who proclaim to you a way of salvation." This went on day after day until Paul got really upset. Following Jesus's example of unwillingness to have evil spirits validate his message (Mark 1:25), Paul commanded, "I order you in the name of Jesus Christ to come out of her!"[5]

Then everything got out of hand. The girl's owners, seeing that their business opportunity was finished, grabbed Paul and Silas and dragged them to the magistrates, probably men with the title of *duumvir*. They then made a provocative accusation – not that Paul and Silas had ruined their business, but that they were "advocating customs that are not lawful for us as Romans to adopt or observe." This accusation, that they were subverting everything the people of Philippi held dear, caused an uproar. With the crowd baying for blood the magistrates quickly ordered Paul and Silas to be "stripped" and "beaten with rods." This was a "severe flogging," which was a technical term distinguishing this punishment from a light beating.[6] This humiliating and extremely painful punishment could never be inflicted on a Roman citizen; but, as far as the magistrates were concerned, the victims were two wandering Jewish preachers of no particular importance. Next, they ordered them to be imprisoned in the "innermost cell," as opposed to the outer cell. The inner cell was dark and filthy, with no toilet arrangements, and was reserved for the more serious villains. The final indignation and disgrace was having their feet fastened in the stocks.[7] As Paul later wrote, they had "suffered and been shamefully mistreated at Philippi" (1 Thess 2:2). For a man in the first century the disgrace would have hurt far more than the physical pain.

The question that immediately arises is why did Paul not claim his Roman citizenship as soon as he was taken before the magistrates. That is what he did later on, in similar circumstances in Jerusalem (Acts 21:39), and it would have been a particularly effective defence in Philippi, where citizenship was such an important issue. Rapske and Hellerman suggest that Paul deliberately laid

---

5. Acts 16:11–18.

6. Brian Rapske, *Paul in Roman Custody,* The Book of Acts in Its First Century Setting, Vol. 3 (Grand Rapids: Eerdmans, 1994), 124.

7. Acts 16:19–24.

aside his rights for the sake of the fledgling church, for if Paul had taken refuge in his citizenship this might have suggested that this new faith was only for citizens. We know that in the early churches most of the believers were not well-to-do citizens, but poor slaves: "Not many were powerful, not many were of noble birth" (1 Cor 1:26). These new believers knew that following Jesus as Messiah would obviously entail risk, so if they needed to be Roman citizens to get protection, then this way would not be viable for them. Paul's commitment to the gospel was so great that he was willing to forego his rights and suffer disgrace and pain, in order that this tiny, new community of believers might have an example they could follow. He laid aside his security and dignity, and took on their place of weakness and dishonour.

Despite all they had been through Paul and Silas were filled with joy. The welts on their backs were bleeding in the stinking darkness, but they kept all the other prisoners awake with their joyful songs of praise! Then at midnight, God suddenly and unexpectedly vindicated them through an earthquake! Everyone's chains fell off, and there could well have been a mass breakout. The jailer was about to commit suicide – because he could not face the disgrace and punishment that would be his for this neglect of duty – when Paul called out that everything was all right. The jailer came to faith, washed their wounds, fed them, and was baptized along with all his household. When the magistrates heard that Paul and Silas were actually Roman citizens they wanted to hush the whole matter up, but Paul now asserted their rights and ensured that they received the public apology they deserved. It was an extraordinary turnaround, and a momentous example and encouragement for the believers. If the God and Father of the Lord Jesus Christ could get Paul out of that predicament, surely he could take care of them too.[8]

Christ's Humiliation and Exaltation

More than ten years later – when Paul was in prison in Rome, writing a letter of friendship and thanksgiving to the church in Philippi – he was still conscious of the challenge of the oppressive Roman culture for the believers. As in Corinth, the highly stratified and competitive Roman model of society was a serious threat to the unity of the church, so a central concern of his letter was to encourage the saints to "do nothing from selfish ambition or conceit, but in humility regard others as better than yourselves" (Phil 2:3). We have already seen how contrary this was to the prevailing world view. Humility was not a positive virtue, but had connotations of the snivelling, obsequious servility

---

8. Acts 16:25–40.

expected of slaves. It was the opposite of the proud self-confidence expected of a Roman gentleman.

In chapter 2, the heart of his letter, Paul reaches for the most powerful argument at his disposal, the example of Christ Jesus, telling the story of his humiliation and exaltation in poetic language:

> who, though he was in the form of God,
> did not regard equality with God
> as something to be exploited,
> but emptied himself,
> taking the form of a slave,
> being born in human likeness.
> And being found in human form,
> he humbled himself
> by becoming obedient to the point of death –
> even death on a cross.
> Therefore, God also highly exalted him
> and gave him the name
> that is above every name,
> so that at the name of Jesus
> every knee should bend,
> in heaven and on earth and under the earth,
> and every tongue should confess
> that Jesus Christ is Lord,
> to the glory of God the Father.

This is the opposite of the *cursus honorum* the Philippians loved to compete in, as it details the downward steps of Christ's humiliation. Before his incarnation, Jesus was in the form of God, his glorious appearance was that of God. The Greek word used for "form" is "*morphe*," which also occurs in Matthew 17:2 to describe his transfiguration, when his true radiance was revealed. The Jewish writer Philo used the same expression "form of God" to describe the emperor Caligula when he dressed up as a god.[9] Because of the debates about Christ's nature in church history we tend to read those questions back into this text. Although the text certainly does have very important implications regarding Christ's being, the context here dictates that the primary focus is his glory and honour. We should not read it to tease out the mysteries of the Chalcedonian creed, about how the two natures of Christ could be united

---

9. Philo of Alexandria, *Embassy to Gaius* (110–114).

in one person, but rather, to understand the significance and influence of the cross on the lives of believers then and now.

Jesus did not regard this equal status with God as something he should cling to and use for himself. Paul's own experience provides a stunning illustration, for he chose not to use his status as a Roman citizen to save himself from suffering and disgrace, but was willing to lay that aside. So Christ Jesus emptied himself of his divine glory, taking on the form and appearance of a slave, the most miserable of men. Roman philosopher Dio Chrysostom said that "slavery is the most shameful and wretched of states."[10] Christ becoming man meant the utter humiliation of a divine being becoming a slave! This was something utterly alien to and incomprehensible for the Romans of Philippi.

The downward movement of self-abasement did not end with the incarnation, but the act of humility took him further, right down as far as anyone could descend – to the cross. Because the cross has now become a respected religious symbol, we struggle to adequately grasp the horror of its original significance.

Martin Hengel's brilliant study of crucifixion in the ancient world contains many terrible accounts that show how common it was.[11] In one instance, a wealthy person found out that one of his slaves had eaten a scrap of fish left over on the dishes he was clearing away after a banquet, and ordered that the man be crucified. The point is that crucifixion was an ordinary, everyday occurrence, and a punishment imposed mainly on slaves. It was routine to see rows of crosses outside Rome, where crucifixions were being carried out by contractors on a commercial basis – the cost of having someone crucified was equivalent to a couple of loaves of bread.

Crucifixion was particularly the punishment for slaves, partly because its purpose was to hold the slave population in fear, but even more, because its true meaning was humiliation. Mocking and torture were normal parts of the process. When the Roman army was besieging Jerusalem in AD 70 and crucifying hundreds of prisoners on the hills around the city, the soldiers took pleasure in nailing their victims in bizarre postures in order to laugh at them. The scourging and mocking that Jesus endured were part of this standard procedure, since the ultimate aim was the degradation and disgrace that all disobedient slaves deserved. This is why the Gospel writers emphasize the injustice and the insults at Jesus's death, but pass over the physical agony; they

---

10. Dio Chrysostom, *1 Serv. lib.* 14.1.

11. Martin Hengel, *Crucifixion* (Philadelphia: Fortress Press, 1977), 55–63.

describe the jeering and catcalls in detail, but make no mention of the searing pain as nails pierced flesh.

For the recipients of this letter in Philippi this must have been profoundly shocking. The Saviour and Son of God whom they were worshipping had willingly chosen to undergo everything that they abhorred and feared. Paul deliberately seeks to overturn their world view, to so disorientate them that they become open to a new paradigm and a new way of living. He was certainly guilty of the accusation brought against him, that he was "advocating customs that are not lawful for us as Romans to adopt or observe." As in Corinth, here in Philippi too, Paul wants to reform the culture of the church, to make it radically different to the society from which it was drawn.

Just as Paul's condemnation by the magistrates was followed by his public vindication, so the death of Jesus was succeeded by his resurrection, with humiliation giving way to exaltation. As he moves on to the final stanza of his poem, Paul again uses the language of honour to describe the significance of the resurrection. God has highly exalted Christ and bestowed on him the name that is above every name, the honour that is above all other honours, so that every being in the whole of creation should acknowledge his glory and sing his praises. "Every knee should bow . . . and every tongue should confess" is a quotation from Isaiah 45:23, where the whole earth admits that Yahweh, the Lord God of Israel, is the only true God, and that salvation is found in him alone. Paul now declares that Jesus is Lord, and that because of his obedience in enduring the shame of the cross he is now restored to the supreme glory of sharing in God's name and honour.

This is Paul's challenge to the members of the church in Philippi, but especially to the leaders. Of all Paul's letters to the churches, only Philippians is specifically addressed to the leaders: "To all the saints in Christ Jesus who are in Philippi, with the bishops and deacons" (Phil 1:1). He knows that the leaders in the church will instinctively continue to lead in the same way they did before their conversion, using their authority to lord it over their followers, building their own reputations at the expense of others, demanding obedience to gild their glory. Leaders who behave like this are denying the core of the gospel, emptying the cross of its meaning. They may gather a group around them, but it will never be a true church that is filled with the power, life and love of the Spirit of Christ.

Paul's *Cursus Honorum*

In chapter 3 of the letter, Paul deals with yet another concern, his fear that the

Philippians might be deceived by the circumcision party – Jewish Christians who were teaching that new Gentile converts should be circumcised and keep the law of Moses if they wanted to become members of the people of God. Paul counters this with his own life story:

> circumcised on the eighth day,
> a member of the people of Israel,
> of the tribe of Benjamin,
> a Hebrew born of Hebrews;
> as to the law, a Pharisee;
> as to zeal, a persecutor of the church;
> as to righteousness under the law, blameless. (Phil 3:5–6)

Hellerman points out that the staccato language reads like an inscription where the mason wants to avoid unnecessary words like verbs as much as possible. The content is remarkably like the *cursus honorum* loved by the people of Philippi, as Paul first describes who he is, and then what he has done. Rather than being of the tribe of the Voltani, he is proud to record he is of the tribe of Benjamin, which proves he is a real Jew. His religious achievements are impressive, and would guarantee respect from the Jewish community. The shocking bombshell comes in verse 8, that he regards all this as *skubalon*, which is variously translated as rubbish, excrement, offscouring, or dregs. He was willing to lose all his standing with the religious Jews in order to gain the far more valuable righteousness that could only be found in Christ. This is Paul's personal version of Christ's humiliation and exaltation described in chapter 2, as Paul too had to forsake his former status as a promising young rabbi, in order to know Christ and gain "the prize of the heavenly call of God in Christ Jesus" (Phil 3:14). He is challenging the Philippian believers to follow suit, by seeing their former social standing as rubbish compared with the glory of knowing Christ, so that they will be able to count their current suffering and rejection a privilege, and start to behave according to their new kingdom values.

This reading of chapter 3 implies that "righteousness" carries a social meaning of belonging to and being honoured among the people of God, rather than the traditional spiritual meaning of standing before God. Since the Reformation, Protestant scholars have agreed that Paul meant that he had been set free from the "works righteousness" of Judaism – the system whereby, in keeping all the commandments and stipulations of the law, they were earning themselves salvation. E. P. Sanders challenged this traditional understanding by surveying the writings of first-century Jewish rabbis and showing that none of them thought they could earn God's favour by keeping the law, and that they all believed they kept the law as a sign that they had been accepted into the covenant people of God. Circumcision, Sabbath and the food laws were a badge, an outward marker of being Jewish.[12]

N. T. Wright and other scholars have built on Sanders's findings to develop the "New Perspective" on Paul, generating many helpful insights.[13] In the letter to the Galatians, Paul's great argument about justification and righteousness is triggered by the incident in which Peter is shamed – by the people who had come down from Jerusalem – into pulling back from eating with the Gentile believers (Gal 2:12). Paul is outraged, because eating together is a key social occasion that expresses acceptance and belonging for everyone at the table. As Peter pulls back from eating with the uncircumcised Gentile converts, the Jewish law of circumcision is being used as the boundary marker that keeps the Gentiles out of fellowship and denies them membership of the people of God. Paul goes on to argue that when Abraham was told to circumcise himself it was a sign that he had believed the promise that "All the Gentiles shall be blessed in you" (Gal 3:8). God's original purpose was for the Gentiles to be blessed by being brought into membership of the people of God; the law of Moses was a temporary arrangement to guide God's people until the Messiah fulfilled the prior promises to Abraham.

John Piper joins other evangelical preachers and scholars in arguing that "righteousness" cannot be divorced from right standing before God.[14] The question whether this can be gained through efforts to keep the religious law, or whether it is only a free gift of God, is vitally important and a central concern for Paul.

I believe these two positions are not mutually exclusive. This may be illustrated by transposing the discussion into the Muslim world. Instead of the Torah there is the Sharia law, but the two are closely linked since Muhammad – clearly borrowing heavily from Jewish teachers he met – included circumcision, food laws with the ban on pork, and washing ceremonies for purification. Works earning favour with God are the basis of Orthodox Islam, which teaches that everyone has two angels, one recording good deeds and the other recording bad deeds, so that at the final judgement good may be weighed against bad. The number of times you pray and fast are counted up in heaven and credited to

---

12. E. P. Sanders, *Paul and Palestinian Judaism* (London: SCM Press, 1977), 419–428.

13. N. T. Wright, *Justification: God's Plan and Paul's Vision* (London: SPCK, 2009), 53–58, 221–224.

14. John Piper, *The Future of Justification* (Wheaton: Crossway, 2007), 183–186.

your account. Every hair that a woman fails to cover with her hijab is recorded and earns her more time in hell.

Performance of Sharia also has significant social consequences. A boy who is not circumcised cannot be considered a Muslim. Failure to keep the food laws means someone is defiled and should be excluded. Joining in the final prayers at the end of the Ramadan fast is an important aspect of being a member of the community. Moreover, there is great honour in keep the Sharia. Older people want to go on the hajj to Mecca – partly as an insurance policy for the judgement that will follow their approaching death, but partly because it gains them great honour. On their return they are given a new title, haji; they gain the right to wear a skull cap that proclaims their new status; and are given places of honour at meals.

Of course, we cannot use Muhammad's example from the seventh century to interpret what Paul meant in the first, but as we minister to Muslims today their understanding certainly affects how we apply the Scriptures to their situation. Coming from a religious mindset that is both legalistic and honour-driven, they need to understand the fullness of what salvation in Christ means for them. They are now accepted as children of God who have been forgiven and are no longer under condemnation, no longer in fear of punishment, and no longer striving to prove themselves. As children of God they are also members of his family, and honoured to bear that title. They no longer need to win honour by putting others down, or protect their own status by excluding others. God's grace transforms the way they relate to God, and to the brothers and sisters who share that grace with them.

5

Jesus and Patronage

God, the Greatest Patron

If a patron is a person with authority who looks after those under him – who in turn offer him their loyalty, respect and service – then clearly the ultimate patron is God himself. As the all-powerful and loving creator of all things, he faithfully sustains his creation and graciously provides for all his creatures. Their only appropriate response to his unmerited generosity is willing obedience, joyful worship, and unstinting service. The deeper their submission to his lordship, the greater their confident delight in his abundant goodness. Since God is the ideal model for all patrons, the Bible does not hesitate to use the language of patron-client relationships to describe God and our relationship to him. In the Hebrew of the Old Testament the common word *kabod* has a root meaning "heavy" – a word used to describe Abram's wealth (Gen 13:2) or the honour of the princes Balak sent to persuade Balaam (Num 22:15). Then, as now, there is a strong link between wealth and honour! But the same word is also used for God's glory (Exod 14:4; Lev 10:3; Deut 28:58), for our honour is a reflection of his glory, as an indicator of superior status and authority.

Similarly, the Greek of the New Testament uses words from the social setting of patronage to help us understand our standing before God. The much-loved word *charis* – which is often used for the grace of God – started out referring to the unmerited and generous favour a patron may bestow on his clients. Aristotle said, "Grace [*charis*] may be defined as helpfulness toward someone in need, not in return for anything..."[1] Those clients should respond to his *charis* with a commitment of faithful loyalty and trust, summed up in the word *pistis*. In the New Testament *pistis* is usually translated "faith" –

---

1. Cited by David A. deSilva, *Honor, Patronage, Kinship & Purity* (Downers Grove: InterVarsity Press, 2000), 104.

which is the only appropriate response to God's grace. This social background to the theological words "grace" and "faith" help us to avoid the mistake of understanding "faith" or "belief" as intellectual assent to dogma, rather than as a living relationship of trusting submission.

Since Jesus is the embodiment of the perfect patron it is not surprising that the vocabulary of patronage is applied to him. When Peter was invited by the Roman centurion Cornelius to present his message it was his first opportunity to preach the gospel to non-Jews. He started by explaining who Jesus was in terms he knew Cornelius would understand. Jesus was someone who "went about doing good" (Acts 10:38). The Greek word for "doing good" is *euergeteo*, which was often used to describe patrons; it is the exact equivalent of the Latin word "*benefactor*," which has passed unchanged into English. Since the Roman Cornelius would have been familiar with the idea and the reality of patronage, Peter describes Jesus as the great patron sent by God to graciously heal and set free all those harshly oppressed and held captive by the dominion of the arch-enemy, the devil.

When patrons addressed their followers they would show respect for their feelings by avoiding demeaning words like "client" – that emphasized inferiority – but instead, often honoured them by calling them "friends." In his great Farewell Discourse in the Upper Room Jesus showed his affection for his disciples by telling them that they were no longer his servants or slaves (*doulos*), but his "friends" (John 15:15). When we read this in English we tend to understand "friends" to mean equality and an easy, informal intimacy. Actually, by using "friends," Jesus is indeed honouring his disciples by affirming his intimacy, but he is not implying a relationship of equal status or suggesting that the disciples should stop showing him all due respect. In the next verse he reminds them that they did not choose him, but he chose them and appointed them to serve him. The Lord is showing great grace by calling his subjects "my friends," but that should not be understood as detracting from his sovereign authority.

Jesus, a Patron of His Time

Jesus lived in a world of hierarchy, shame and honour, where space carried social meaning. Once, when invited to eat at the home of a high-ranking leader of the Pharisees, he noticed how the other guests were vying with one another to sit in the places of honour, near the top of the table (Luke 14:7–11). The guests were not simply looking for a conveniently empty seat, but were acutely aware of the gradation of honour, starting at the bottom nearest the door, and ascending to the top where the host sat. Sitting as near the top as possible was vitally important, and led to some scarcely concealed elbowing others out of the way. Jesus seized the opportunity to tell them a parable, and we can imagine him saying, "When you come to a banquet like this don't try to sit at the top, but sit at the bottom. If you consider yourself better than the other guests and push yourself to the top, just think how humiliated you will feel when the host tells you to make way for someone more important than yourself, and you have to go down to the bottom with everyone else watching you! Conversely, imagine the pride you will feel if your host calls you further up the table and calls you 'friend' in front of all the other guests."

Westerners hearing this parable miss much of its significance because, for them, seating arrangements are usually a matter of convenience and not of status. When we come into a room we look for empty seats or seats next to the friends we want to talk to. But Iranian friends have told me how awkward they felt when they first attended a Bible study and had to find a seat in a room full of strangers. They knew who the teacher was, and so knew where the most honoured seats were; however, since they did not know the age or seniority of the other students they did not know where to place themselves in the pecking order, which meant they could face the same disgrace of being moved to the bottom that Jesus talked about in his parable. When we were new missionaries in Turkey my wife quickly learnt her place as the hostess. Whereas I was the host, and sat on the opposite side of the room from the door, her responsibility was to keep everyone's tea glasses full and so she sat by the door ready to go to her place in the kitchen!

Jesus lived in this world of shame, honour and patronage, but he turned it upside down. He helpfully spells out the meaning of his parable: "For all who exalt themselves will be humbled, and those who humble themselves will be exalted" (Luke 14:11). He is redefining honour, not as the praise and respect of men, but as the praise and affirmation of God. The honour of this world is temporary and deceptive, and ultimately founded on a lie. God is the true source of honour, and good standing in God's eyes is the greatest honour that we should all be seeking.

People understood Jesus to be a patron because, in many ways, he behaved like one; but he rejected the fundamental premise on which the world's patronage system was founded. All four Gospels record his response to the huge crowd that came out into the countryside to hear his teaching and ask for healing for their sick. Even though he had just heard that his cousin John the Baptist had been murdered – a forewarning of his own death – he had compassion on them, and gave himself to meeting their physical and spiritual needs. When evening came he realized they had not eaten all day, and that the walk back to buy food would be hard for them. Acting as a true patron, he took responsibility for their needs by feeding them with just five loaves of bread and two fish. The crowd recognized that this miracle was a sign that he was "the prophet who is to come into the world," but they interpreted it through the lens of their own understanding of leadership and patronage (John 6:14–15). They were ready to proclaim him their king, in exchange for a steady supply of bread, rather like the Roman mob who shouted Nero's praises as long as he gave them bread and circuses. They would accept Jesus's authority and accord him great titles if, in exchange, he looked after them and guaranteed them a secure food supply.

Jesus knew that his kingdom was not of this world, and that the crowd's offer of kingship had nothing to do with his messianic mission, so he simply disappeared up the mountain by himself. He could have enjoyed power and popular acclaim but he walked away from it. When the crowd found him again the next day they were still looking for bread (John 6:26, 34). He tested them, teaching them the true nature of his kingdom – that he himself was "the bread of life" (6:35) and that "unless you eat the flesh of the Son of Man and drink his blood, you have no life in you" (John 6:53). The crowd melted away and he was left with just his small band of disciples. For Roman patrons, the measure of their honour was the number of people in their retinue. For Jesus, the adulation of large numbers of people did not matter, but rather, knowing his Father's pleasure.

Jesus Rejects Worldly Patronage

Again and again Jesus had to choose between the world's leadership model of patronage and the authority of his Father's kingdom. One of his greatest tests came just after his baptism – at which the Holy Spirit settled on him like a dove and the voice from heaven declared that he was the beloved Son of God, with whom the Father was well pleased (Matt 3:17). This fulfilled the prophecy of Psalm 2, that the anointed Messiah (v. 2), the king reigning in Zion (v. 6), would be the Son of God come to take the nations as his heritage and possession (v. 8). With this great promise ringing in his ears Jesus went into the desert to be tempted by the devil, with a furious assault on his God-given identity (Matt 4:1–11). Twice Satan tried to use guile: "If you are the Son of God, command these stones to become loaves of bread," and "If you are the Son of God, throw yourself down; for it is written, 'He will command his angels concerning you.'" Seeing that these attempts were in vain, Satan resorted to a direct attack, offering Jesus all the kingdoms of the world and their glory if he would only fall down in worship. Luke writes that Satan showed Jesus "all the kingdoms of the world" and offered him "their glory and all this authority" (Luke 4:5–6).

At his baptism, his Father had quoted from Psalm 2 to promise Jesus the nations; now Satan was promising him the nations, with all their glory and authority. We may wonder whether Satan really could or would deliver on that promise, but at that moment Jesus had a decisive choice: would he inherit the nations by obeying his Father, using his Father's authority in his Father's way, and then being rewarded with his Father's glory? Or would he pay homage to Satan, bowing to his authority, receiving Satan's authority to do his work? To whom would he submit and in whose name would he exercise authority and power? Whose glory would he seek? Jesus's reply was immediate, unhesitating and unequivocal: "Away with you, Satan! for it is written, 'Worship the Lord your God, and serve only him'" (Matt 4:10). Jesus chose the path of obedience, humility and service. In our lives, too, the most important decision is to whom we will submit; we all submit and give allegiance to some person or ideology, and if we say we submit to no one we are deceiving ourselves. Actually, if we proudly assert we are submitting to no one, then we are seeking to enthrone ourselves, and so doing exactly what Satan wants us to do!

Satan wanted Jesus to bow in worship before him, and in so doing to become his client on whom he would bestow his favours. The Greek word here for worship is *proskunesis*, literally "bowing to kiss the hand." This word often occurs in the Septuagint – the Greek translation of the Old Testament – and almost always refers to the worship of God. In the book of Esther, however, it is used to describe the practice of the Persian court – for example, when the servants of King Ahasuerus bowed down and paid homage to the wicked Haman, the word used is *proskunesis* (Esth 3:2).

About 150 years after Esther the practice of *proskunesis* became highly controversial. In 328 BC Alexander the Great was campaigning to conquer what is now northern Afghanistan. One evening, as was his usual custom, he held a drinking party with his companions. This time, however, there was a difference, as Alexander had everyone present drink in turn from a cup of wine, propose a toast, and then perform *proskunesis* to him. Alexander had defeated Darius and captured Persepolis two years earlier in 330 BC, and was being progressively influenced by Persian culture and customs. Increasing numbers of Persians were becoming courtiers, and they would naturally prostrate and kiss their hands to show obeisance to their new ruler. Alexander now wanted the veterans who had come with him all the way from Macedonia to do the same.[2]

One by one they rose and did as asked, until it was the turn of Callisthenes – a great-nephew of Aristotle – who had joined the army as official historian and was a true defender of Greek culture and values. As long as Alexander was humiliating the barbarian Persians he was happy to eulogize him, but now that he was adopting their customs Callisthenes was having second thoughts. For Greeks, *proskunesis* was only performed in worship to the gods, and for a Greek to do so to a man was deeply humiliating. It is doubtful whether Alexander really wanted to be worshipped as a god, and was probably more concerned that all his officers follow the same norms. He was trying to deal with the acute clash of cultures between the egalitarian West and the hierarchical East. Callisthenes's refusal to honour Alexander with *proskunesis* ended their relationship, and shortly afterwards he was implicated as the instigator of a failed assassination plot to be carried out by some pages he had been mentoring. Callisthenes was savagely executed, and Alexander's friendship with his teacher Aristotle was broken forever. Conflicting views of culture and authority were as dangerous then as they are today.

Bowing and kissing the hand is still prevalent in Asia. For Turkish children it is a happy custom to respectfully kiss their grandparents' hands and be rewarded with sweets or pocket money. Tragically, British prisoners of war were savagely beaten by their Japanese captors during the Second World War because they refused to kowtow before them. To the Japanese, the refusal to bow was a sign of arrogant disrespect; to the British, it was one humiliation too many. My point is not that one culture or world view is better than another, but that for Jesus, bowing in worship before Satan would have been an expression of submission to his authority and acceptance of his values.

In Psalm 2, the rulers of the earth are warned to serve the Lord and "kiss his feet, or he be angry" (Ps 2:12). Since Jesus rejected Satan's offer and continued to perfectly fulfil his Father's will, he has been given the nations, their authority and their glory. Now it is their kings who must decide if they will cling to their own authority or accept his reign by serving and worshipping him. The latter decision results in experiencing the Son's blessing, the former in suffering his wrath.

---

2. Robin Lane Fox, *Alexander the Great* (New York: Penguin, 1973), 320–325.

Political Honour

Jesus repeatedly warned his disciples not to conform to the world's understanding of authority, honour and power. Like everyone else, they assumed that Jesus's messianic kingdom was going to be one of great political power and military might that would defeat the hated Roman oppressors and usher in a government of righteousness and peace. Excitement grew as Jesus set out on his final journey to Jerusalem. The disciples began to speculate about what roles they might have in the new regime. James and John were cousins of Jesus – sons of his aunt Salome – and so they anticipated some key positions. Together with their mother they approached Jesus to ask him for the second and third most powerful positions in his kingdom, the seats on his right and his left (Matt 20:20–28; Mark 10:35–45). In today's terms, they wanted to be the Minister of Finance and the Minister of Defence. They wanted to share in his glory, which they would have understood to mean the status, the financial resources, the large retinue of hangers-on, and the perks of office. When the other ten disciples heard about this ploy they were understandably furious. Jesus gathered them all together and rebuked them for wanting to be like the Gentiles. Their rulers "lord it over" their subjects, bossing them around in order to show off their power and position. They love to exercise authority over them in a harsh, controlling and dominating way. They compete for high office so they can enjoy prestige. The kingdom of heaven is utterly different, because greatness lies in service and the desire to excel should result in being a slave to all. This is how Jesus himself understood his mission – that he came not to be served but to serve, to the extent of giving his life as a ransom for many.

Religious Honour

Jesus reserved his strongest criticism for the religious elite, because their use of God's name and authority to promote themselves was the most toxic form of leadership abuse. After his arrival in Jerusalem, Jesus drove the moneychangers out of the temple, provoking his last great confrontation with the scribes and Pharisees. At the end of an extended debate with them, he silenced them by showing them that the Son of David is none other than God himself, and then turned on them with stinging condemnation (Matt 23:1–12).

His chief charge against them was hypocrisy, one of his main criticisms of them from the beginning. They preached one thing, but did the opposite. They demanded that others carry heavy burdens which they themselves neither carried nor helped others to carry. They were experts in the law of Moses, skilled in analyzing and interpreting verses, and persuasive in teaching the commands to others. They were great in the study and the pulpit, but thought their knowledge and oratory was enough. Since their lives did not and could not match their preaching, their words became a poisonous lie. They excelled at religious performance, brilliant at praying long, impressive prayers (Mark 12:40) and making a show of their spirituality. The real motivation for all this piety was their hunger for honour and respect. Of course, they would have angrily denied such an accusation, and maybe they themselves were not aware of just how much of their behaviour was driven by the desire to be praised by men.

When our religion goes public on a platform, we are in danger, for from that moment it inevitably starts to be a performance. Being on a platform it is quite right that we learn the skills of presentation, how to project our voices, how to engage the audience, how to fashion our message to be persuasive and effective. The danger is that we may also look for the applause, and enjoy our new-found prominence. Whether we acknowledge it or not, our egos enjoy being puffed up, and so we develop our platform presence. Sermons get longer and worship in front of others becomes more intense as we subconsciously respond to the attention we are attracting. We may not even realize what is happening until we are criticized or someone else is given the limelight instead of us – and then our angry or jealous reaction should wake us up to the truth behind our religious zeal. We tell ourselves and everyone else it is for God, but actually it is for ourselves.

For the scribes and Pharisees, the honour they desired so much was expressed in titles. The examples Jesus gives are rabbi, father and instructor (Matt 23:7–10). For us in the egalitarian West today this is not much of a problem, because in our love of informality we have largely stopped respecting one another with titles. My grandfather would address even his old lifelong friends by their surname, prefaced by "mister." Today, children call their parents by their first names.

The principal of the Bible college where I met my wife Lenna was Rev Dr Geoffrey Grogan, affectionately known to students as "the gentle giant" because of his six-foot, six-inch height, and with a national reputation for his scholarly, staunch and yet gracious stand for evangelical truth. He officiated at our wedding and, when we returned to Scotland after fifteen years of living in Turkey, we met up again.

"How are you, Mr Grogan?" I enquired.

"Oh, please call me Geoff," he replied, obviously embarrassed by the formality of my address.

"I can't possibly call you Geoff," I countered, "You are the man who taught us and then married us."

After all that time in the Middle East it was unthinkable not to express my respect for him with a suitable title.

When I was in Ankara the younger Turkish believers used to call me *ağabey* (big brother). As I got older they affectionately teased me by calling me *amca* (uncle). This came from healthy respect and signified how close they felt to me. I don't think Jesus was telling his disciples to stop using kinship terms to honour their elders, but as someone who grew up in a culture based on shame and honour he was warning them of the subtle danger of desiring such titles to promote self-importance. When the titles become a source of pleasure and pride, something to be flaunted to put others down, then they have become tainted and corrupting.

Jesus went on to pronounce seven woes of judgement against the scribes and Pharisees (Matt 23:13–36) because their use of religion to pursue their own honour had disastrous consequences for the people they should have been ministering to. Jesus accused them of locking people out of the kingdom of heaven because they had become such a stumbling block in the way of those who were spiritually hungry. They expended great effort to win a single proselyte from a Gentile background, probably because of the way it would enhance their own reputations, but then left him in an even bigger mess than themselves. They were blind guides, leading people astray. Finally, they became murderers, killing the prophets, sages and scribes who threatened their comfortable kingdom by proclaiming the true word of God.

Before we judge the scribes and Pharisees for their failures, we must look carefully at ourselves, to see to what extent we sit in their seat. I have already mentioned how poor leadership in Bulgaria and Central Asia resulted in a decimation of the church. We rejoice over the new believers who join us from a Muslim background, but to what extent are we to blame for the large numbers who leave? Of course, there are many who come with mixed motives, and others who turn aside when they realize the cost of discipleship. Yet, too often we hear from people that they left because of their disillusionment with the church. They were attracted by the message of the love of God and the amazing grace-filled life of Jesus, and expected the church to be a community full of that same spirit. Instead, they say, they found hypocrisy and self-interest, and often their most biting complaint is against the leaders. Sometimes, we have won a convert, but at the end of the story he is out of work, estranged from his family, angry at God and embittered at the church – "twice as much a child of hell." How important it is that we ask God to humble our hearts, so that no pursuit of honour for ourselves would ever result in disgrace for his name.

Squabbling to the End

The extraordinary thing is that, despite having lived with Jesus for three years and listened to his teaching, the disciples had still not understood his message. Just after Jesus instituted the Last Supper, explaining that bread signified his body and the wine his blood, they started arguing about who was the greatest (Luke 22:24–27). He had just told them that one of them would betray him, and perhaps their discussion about the betrayer turned into mutual accusations, and then descended into a dispute about who was the greatest. Their self-centredness is astonishing. Maybe they had not understood the seriousness of the crisis that was about to break, and were still dreaming about sitting on Jesus's right hand or his left. Yet again Jesus had to remind them of what he had already taught them – that this desire to lord it over others and to collect titles like "benefactor" or "patron" was a characteristic of the Gentiles. Among the true people of God the greatest is the one who does not go after status and serves others, just like Jesus.

Despite the disciples' continued failure to grasp the essential nature of his kingdom, Jesus affirmed them and expressed his confidence in them. He promised them the privilege of sitting with him at his table in his kingdom. He also said they would share in his kingdom authority by playing a role in the coming judgement (Luke 22:28–30). Although they still thought the exercise of authority was meant to add lustre to their standing and status, Jesus told them that in the future they would be trusted to exercise true authority with the wisdom and impartial justice needed to act as judges.

How could Jesus be sure of this? How would this profound transformation of their hearts come about? How do people change?

6

Jesus and His Disciples

Changing Their Deepest Assumptions

Some things are easy to learn, and some are very difficult. It is easy to learn a new piece of information like a phone number, or a new skill like a recipe. It is much harder to learn to be patient, to think differently, to see the world in a new way. Our understanding of authority develops while we are still small children, as we watch how family members relate to one another, and especially to our fathers. How approachable is he? Is he kind and generous? How much do others defer to him? Are they afraid of him?

These early impressions significantly influence the way we think of leadership. Since our later understanding is built on early experiences that are buried deep in our subconscious, it is difficult to change the way we think, or even to be aware of why we behave as we do. Later in life, we may learn about different attitudes and give intellectual assent to new ideas, but in moments of crisis, and under stress, the older, deeper framework reasserts itself. As we saw with the disciples, three years of listening to Jesus's teaching, and even watching his example, was not enough to change their fundamental assumption that leadership is about controlling others in order to win honour and build reputation. If teaching and example by themselves were not enough, how did Jesus change them?

One day the disciples came to Jesus and asked him who was the greatest in the kingdom of heaven (Matt 18:1–5). Peter had already declared that Jesus was the Messiah, and they were on their way up to Jerusalem for the last time. They had started to think politically, calculating who would occupy which position when the Messiah liberated Jerusalem from the Roman yoke: "Who is the greatest? Who is your favourite? Who will be your lieutenant?" Jesus called a child, and put him among them. Having drawn their attention to the little one and provoked their curiosity, he told them they had to change in order to enter God's kingdom. They had to humble themselves like a little child in order to be the greatest. They were stunned by his disconcerting reply, because children were neither powerful nor honoured, and to put humility and greatness in the same sentence was a meaningless oxymoron. They were probably so nonplussed by his response that they shrugged their shoulders and quickly forgot it.

Transformative Learning

Over the last thirty years students of adult education have become increasingly interested in transformative learning – learning that results in profound and permanent shifts in attitudes and behaviour, as opposed to merely acquiring knowledge and skills. Jack Mezirow, the pioneer in this field, formulated the theory that for personal transformation to occur there had to be a disorienting dilemma – a situation that previously held paradigms could not explain, and that produced confusion and distress. Only this can lead to the open, searching, critical reflection of previously held assumptions that is necessary for radical rethinking, and thus lead to a sustainable, irreversible change of self-image, world view, roles and relationships.[1]

Jesus's response to the disciples' question is an example of a disorienting dilemma. When the disciples asked about greatness they were thinking of power, wealth and honour. By making them look at a child – who may have been loved, but had no position of significance or influence – Jesus compelled them to bring together the contradictory concepts of weakness and power. He was setting up a situation that challenged their assumptions and called into question their view of leadership.

Jesus often used paradox to set up these disorienting dilemmas. I count thirteen verses in which the gospel writers record him saying either "the first will be last" or "the least shall be the greatest" or "he who exalts himself will be humbled." In addition to his references to children,[2] Jesus concludes the encounter with the rich young man by saying, "But many who are first will be last, and the last will be first."[3] Similar teaching is reported seven times, all occurring towards the end of his ministry, on the final journey from Galilee

---

1. Jack Mezirow, "Learning to Think Like an Adult: Core Concepts of Transformation Theory," in *Learning as Transformation: Critical Perspectives on a Theory in Progress*, edited by Jack Mezirow et al. (San Francisco: Jossey-Bass, 2000), 22.

2. Matt 18:4; Mark 9:35; Luke 9:48.

3. Matt 19:30; Mark 10:31.

up to Jerusalem.[4] As the end drew nearer the jealousies among the disciples grew more intense, and Jesus foresaw the problems this could cause after his departure.

The incident where James and John come with their mother (Matt 20:20) to ask Jesus for positions of authority on his right hand and left is revealing. Jesus's initial rebuke reminded them that the way to authority and influence in his Father's kingdom was through drinking the cup he was going to drink, which means they would have to suffer like him. We then read that the other ten were angry, which raises the question of how they knew about the ploy of the two brothers. Presumably the two would not have had the gall to ask for this preferential treatment in front of the ten, so it must be that Jesus rebuked the two in the hearing of the ten. He deliberately provoked a conflict among the twelve in order to create a disorienting dilemma, a painful situation that exposed the flaws in their world view as well as in their characters. He may have done this in part to show them the damage done by intrigue like this, but mainly to open up the opportunity to teach a vital truth. The rulers of this world lord it over others and use their authority to domineer and control, but the followers of Jesus must be servants and slaves of one another.

Although Mezirow's theory of transformative learning has been widely accepted, many writers have highlighted areas of weakness that need further research. Edward Taylor echoed their views when he observed that because Mezirow was American he viewed transformative learning as a rational process followed by an individual, and did not pay enough attention to the emotional, experiential and communal aspects.[5] The way Jesus dealt with the whole group struck me forcefully, because I, as a Westerner, would have taken James and John aside privately to avoid an unseemly confrontation. Jesus, however, understood the importance of dealing with the situation in community, because what is learnt together with others is learnt more deeply and retained longer. The added dimensions of group accountability and the heightened emotional impact strengthen the effectiveness of the learning.

An outstanding example of Jesus using a disorienting dilemma to undermine his disciples' presuppositions is when he washed their feet (John 13:1–20). The time of his departure is now very near, and he knows that the issue of their rivalry for positions has still not been settled, so he resorts to an even more drastic approach. They are gathered to celebrate the Passover,

---

4. Matt 20:16; 23:11–12; Mark 10:43–44; Luke 13:30; 14:11; 18:14; 22:26.

5. Edward W. Taylor, "Building Upon the Theoretical Debate: A Critical Review of the Empirical Studies of Mezirow's Transformative Learning Theory," *Adult Education Quarterly* 48 (1997): 34–59.

the most solemn and sacred meal in the Jewish calendar. There is a sense of foreboding in the air as everyone is aware that the final confrontation with the authorities is imminent. Suddenly Jesus gets up, takes off his robe, picks up a towel and ties it around his waist, and pours water into a basin. Then he kneels down before his disciples, and begins to wash their feet and wipe them with the towel. This was the duty of the lowest servant in the house, and the disciples are utterly disoriented by this reversal of roles. They feel profoundly embarrassed and ashamed that their master is doing this, for any disgrace he suffers affects his followers as well. They are caught in the dilemma of whether or not to allow him to continue. Impetuous Peter can take it no longer, and when Jesus reaches him he protests, "You will never wash my feet!" Jesus replies, "Unless I wash you, you have no share with me."

There is an echo here of an earlier incident (Matt 16:13–23). Peter has just declared that Jesus is the Messiah, and Jesus then warns the disciples that he will suffer and be killed. On that occasion, too, Peter protests, "This must never happen to you," and Jesus's response is even harsher: "Get behind me, Satan!" Jesus washing his disciples' feet is a foreshadowing of the cross – in both cases, his humiliation leads to cleansing for his disciples. As we will see, his crucifixion was the ultimate disorienting dilemma.

The cross and the foot washing both serve to create a new community. As Jesus took the basin and the towel, he was disrupting the default assumptions of their culture, so that they would be ready to receive his instruction to wash one another's feet, and to obey his new commandment to love one another as he had loved them (John 13:34). The success of Jesus's mission after he returned to his Father depended on the unity of his followers – and that unity would soon fragment if they were going to compete for prominence.

In this example, we also see the importance of experience for transformative learning. Lived experience is much more likely to produce a dissonance that is strong enough to cause serious questioning of established and accepted paradigms. For instance, medical students may be sent to a hospice to spend time with the terminally ill and their families, in order to help them learn empathy. Educators understand that powerful emotional experiences have a significant influence on entrenched attitudes.

Mentoring

Supportive relationships are another dimension that commentators like Taylor add to Mezirow's model. A disorienting dilemma is more likely to result in transformation if it is grounded in a powerful experience, processed in a community, and then the subsequent reflection is encouraged through a supportive relationship.

Mentoring is critical for leadership development and personal growth, and is exemplified supremely by Jesus's relationship with his disciples. Jesus called people to follow him, to become his disciples, and in so doing they were submitting to God's reign and entering his kingdom. He called them to leave their old lives behind "to be with him" (Mark 3:14), to be his constant companions, to eat, travel and minister with him. The mutual bonds of love and commitment provided the platform for the teaching, training in ministry, and inner change that equipped the disciples to continue Jesus's mission after he had left them.

Whereas Jesus calls people to follow, Paul exhorts them to imitate. This is not surprising, since Paul was responsible for extending the Great Commission into the Gentile world – where the concept of imitation was common among the Greek philosophers. Aristotle wrote about its importance: "it is an instinct of human beings, from childhood, to engage in mimesis (imitation) . . . and it is through imitation that he develops his earliest understanding."[6] It was expected that children would imitate their parents, students their teachers, and subjects their rulers. Xenophon wrote of Cyrus that he "set before his subjects a perfect model of virtue in his own person."[7] Philosophers like Aristotle or Plato would gather groups of students, who would spend hours in their company in order to imbibe their values and customs. Nor was this restricted to the Hellenistic world, as Jewish rabbis adopted a similar strategy with their disciples, who would deliberately mimic every trait of their mentor and model.

The idea of "imitating" occurs most frequently in the letters to the Thessalonians and in 1 Corinthians. Paul has just arrived in Europe and is wrestling with the issues raised by new converts from pagan backgrounds. The most pressing problem is the persecution they are suffering, which is threatening to destroy their new faith. Paul commends them for imitating the worthy examples of Paul and Silas, the Lord Jesus himself, and the churches in Judea (1 Thess 1:6; 2:14). The believers in Thessalonica are experiencing the joy of the Holy Spirit, and Paul uses these examples to reassure them that their suffering is neither in vain nor because they have made a mistake. Their suffering is like that of Jesus and the apostles, and therefore noble and righteous.

Second, the lifestyles of the new believers are still deeply influenced by their pagan backgrounds, and they will learn their new way of living by imitating

---

6. Aristotle, *Poetics* IV.

7. Xenophon, *Cyr.* 8.22.

Paul. Some of them are tempted to consider their new faith an excuse for idleness, so Paul reminds them how he worked day and night "so that we might not burden any of you" and "in order to give you an example to imitate" (2 Thess 3:8–9). In Corinth, the old idea of wisdom being proud and boastful is leading to division, so Paul graphically describes his own weakness and humility as the pattern they are to imitate (1 Cor 4:9–16). New believers need to see the new life lived out by authentic and relevant models.

When we lived in Turkey in the 1980s we would take our new converts to an annual national Christian camp. For these new believers it was their first opportunity to meet mature national leaders and to ask the questions we had been unable to answer. I remember one brother exclaiming, "Now I know what it means to live as a Christian!" At that time, the leaders were still from minority Christian backgrounds, like Armenians or Assyrians, but they were still culturally much closer than we Westerners. Suddenly our new brother met a model of Christian living he could relate to, and could imagine himself emulating.

Third, Paul gives us an example to imitate in the depth and intensity of his mentoring relationships. Like a nursing mother, he cares so deeply for his protégés that along with the gospel he is willing to share his own self (1 Thess 2:7–8). He is "like a father with his children, urging and encouraging you and pleading that you lead a life worthy of God" (1 Thess 2:11–12). He loves them passionately, is willing to give whatever is necessary to see them established in the Lord, and shares his whole life with them so that they can imitate his attitudes and not just mimic his actions. I believe the deeper the heart-to-heart connection, the greater the transfer of values.

While living in Istanbul I had the privilege of meeting Bishop Mesrop Mutafyan, Patriarch of the Armenian Orthodox Church. He told me about a problem he faced when the Turkish government would not allow the church to have a seminary to train priests. So he was compelled to send his young men either to the theologically liberal Sorbonne in Paris or to a nationalistic institution in Yerevan, Armenia. Despite these unfortunate circumstances he was happy to report that his students returned from their studies abroad still faithful to his principles. Remembering the weaknesses and failure of so much of our discipleship of Turkish believers I was eager to hear his secret.

"How do you manage to ground them so well that they stay faithful to your spirituality?" I asked.

"It's easy," he replied. "They live with me for three years! They eat with me, sit with me, talk with me, hang out with me." Then he added with a smile, "Of course, for you Protestants that is difficult because you get married! We Orthodox bishops remain celibate so that we can devote ourselves to raising up the next generation."

Fourth, this mentoring relationship includes an element of authority. In 1 Corinthians 4, Paul admonishes them as a father (v. 14), appeals to them to imitate him (v. 16), and then goes so far as to raise the possibility that he may come to them with a stick (v. 21). Some have accused Paul of a power play, of abusing his authority in a coercive way to force the Corinthians to comply with his agenda. But Paul is calling them to imitate himself in his weakness, humility and suffering, not asking them to accord him a special position or privilege. It is noteworthy that the word "disciple" never occurs in the New Testament after the book of Acts. The disciples are the followers of Jesus, and so Paul never claims to have his own disciples. In the Great Commission we are told to "make disciples" by baptizing people into the name of the Trinity and by teaching them to obey all the commands of Jesus (Matt 28:19–20). They commit themselves to the Father, Son and Holy Spirit, and to obey all the commands of the Lord Jesus Christ. They are *his* disciples, not ours. According to Paul, they may be called our spiritual children – for we led them to faith – or our co-workers, as they now serve alongside us. But they are not our followers, for we do not have absolute authority over them; we do not own them.

Nevertheless, there is a voluntary submission to Paul's apostolic authority. Paul directs the members of his ministry team and gives instructions to the churches. He does not dominate, coerce or exploit, but rather lays down his life to serve them. As they heed his admonishments, carry out his instructions, and take his life as their model to imitate, they will become more and more like him, just as Paul's goal is to become more and more like Christ. This does not mean that their individuality is obliterated or that they become clones of Paul, but they too grow in the likeness of Christ as their unique calling finds expression in his kingdom as members of his body in all its diversity.

Jesus and Paul provide us with a model of how to mentor people into transformation, set free from the constraints of their culture to conform to the values of Christ. This is how they can move beyond being honour-driven patrons into the servant leadership of Jesus. It will take mentors who open up their lives in committed relationships, sharing their suffering and sorrows, encouraging and admonishing as needed. They will shepherd others through the experience of disorienting dilemmas on to searching reflection and the discovery of new perspectives, in the context of community. The reward is students who surpass their teachers.

Jesus and Paul recruited young men, and there is no doubt that youth finds this transformation easier and can make more rapid progress. When I joined OM International and went to India at the age of twenty-two, I found myself immersed in a very different culture. I had the privilege of being the only Westerner on an evangelistic team of Indians, and soon became used to walking down the street holding hands with the guys, and sharing one of my few shirts with whoever needed it. We lived by selling gospel literature, so when sales were low food was scarce; occasionally, angry Hindus threw a few stones at us. As we endured these hardships, we grew even closer to one another. Most significantly, I was under the leadership of Indians, unusual for white missionaries back then. S. N. Das had been a corporal in the Indian army, decorated for bravery fighting the Chinese, while Resham Raj was a Nepali from a Brahmin background, who had memorized the Gospel of Luke while in prison. They were gifted leaders, with very definite ideas about how the team should be run. There was not a lot of consultation when they announced we were getting up at 5:00 a.m. for early morning prayer or that Friday was going to be a day of prayer and fasting. They were deeply godly men, and to this day both are still active in Christian ministry. For a recently saved semi-hippy like myself it was a life-changing experience, as I learnt resilience and perseverance. Most of all I learnt the discipline of submission to leaders from a different cultural background, who combined Christ-like character with a strong sense of the authority that had been invested in them. To a large extent, it made me who I am today. Leadership development is a long-term process, and there is no doubt that the sooner it is started the better.

Of course, this does not mean only young people can be mentored and trained. Mature men and women from a more hierarchical cultural background may well struggle with difficulties and disappointments in their leadership. Divisions and discouragements take a heavy toll, and yet these times of darkness can be the disorienting dilemma that opens up new horizons. I have observed established pastors who tended to be controlling or overbearing becoming servant leaders over time, through the experience of failure. Whereas seminars and workshops by well-meaning teachers may have only a limited influence, a trusted mentor, who comes alongside in a time of despair, can help find the way to a new model of a more gracious leadership style, that gives more space to the weak who are struggling or to enthusiastic young believers who are keen to develop their own ministries.

The Crucifixion

Despite three years with the greatest mentor who has ever lived, observing the example of his life from the privileged perspective of an intimate friendship, at the Last Supper the disciples were still arguing about who was the greatest (Luke 22:24)! Despite Jesus's masterly training programme – with its unique blend of teaching, experience, community and disorientation – their deeply rooted cultural default of competing for honour had still not been eradicated. Had Jesus failed? Would his mission fall apart as soon as he left them?

Jesus still had one more move. He had repeatedly warned the disciples that he would be crucified, but because of their fixed mindset they had failed to understand or really believe it. As Peter had twice objected, the Messiah must come as a glorious conqueror, not suffer as a servant. Suffering and death was literally unthinkable. The very night of their argument about who was the greatest, their world collapsed. A few hours later, they turned tail and fled when the soldiers came to arrest Jesus in Gethsemane, and Peter denied his Lord three times. The next day, Jesus was condemned on trumped-up charges, scourged, mocked, spat on, stripped, and nailed to a cross in-between two thieves. It seems that none of his disciples, except John, had the courage to go to the cross, and it was the women who stood there as witnesses, to pass on to us an account of those dreadful events.

The Romans had inflicted on Jesus the ultimate punishment of a slave, with the degrading taunts and mockery intended to utterly humiliate. All Jesus's words about humility, servanthood and slavery were suddenly embodied in his bloodied corpse hanging on the cross. He died, while they went free.

The phrase "disorienting dilemma" is not strong enough to describe the depths of anguish and despair the disciples suffered. First, there was their own personal failure to stand with their Lord because of their cowardice, despite all their boasts that they were ready to die for him. It must have been a devastating blow to their pride. More serious was the failure of their theology and belief system, as the power and glory they were building their hopes on turned to weakness and disgrace. Their mental constructs crashed as their inner worlds disintegrated.

Yet it was not the end for the disciples. Jesus rose from the dead. He appeared to them and lovingly restored them. He came to Peter by the lake, as he had done at the beginning, and renewed his commission (John 21:15–19). He explained to them again how these things had to happen because they were written in the Scriptures, and this time their minds were open so they could understand and grasp what he was saying (Luke 24:45). He gave them the gift of his Holy Spirit to empower them for all that lay ahead.

Significantly, the disciples never again squabbled about who was the greatest or competed with one another for pre-eminence. They did have lengthy, spirited discussions about vital questions like the circumcision of

Gentile converts, but at the Council of Jerusalem we see how they were able to resolve differences by listening respectfully to one another and to the Scriptures (Acts 15:7, 12). Although Peter took the lead in dealing with Ananias and Sapphira (Acts 5:1–11), and later James acts as spokesman and chairman to draw the discussion at the Council to a close (Acts 15:13–21), it is clear that the disciples shared leadership and made decisions together. It was "the twelve" who decided to ask the community to appoint seven men of good standing to oversee the distribution of food to the widows (Acts 6:1–7). The cross finally achieved what three years of training had been preparing the disciples for – their transformation.

For Jesus, the cross was the doorway to the resurrection and ascension, when he returned to his Father and was crowned with glory and honour. The promises of Psalm 2 and the heavenly voice at his baptism were fulfilled as the Son entered into his kingdom and was given the nations as his inheritance.

Mark and John record how, at the trial of Jesus, the soldiers mocked him by placing a crown of thorns on his head and a robe of purple around his shoulders. He had claimed to be a king, but he had no recognizable majesty or authority and so they ridiculed his kingship with the purple. Above his head was the ironic sign, "King of the Jews" (John 19:19). Unlike Constantine, who could not bring himself to give up the purple, Jesus had never sought the purple and had deliberately turned down empty honours. He truly did "give up the purple," renouncing any claim to worldly royalty.

Today, in some liturgical churches, purple is used as the colour of Easter. This is clearly a reference to the purple robe of majesty that was used to mock Jesus before he was crucified. But it may also carry a deeper meaning when we remember that purple is a mixture of blue and red. Blue signifies the man come from heaven; red reminds us of his blood and suffering. His kingdom was established when the divine Son of God humbled himself to "death on a cross," and was given an authority and glory that will one day be universally acknowledged.

Psalm 110 tells us that the Son is now seated on the throne at his Father's right hand, waiting for his enemies to become his footstool, put under his feet in disgrace. The Son will be vindicated, given "the name that is above every name, so that at the name of Jesus every knee should bend . . . and every tongue should confess that Jesus Christ is Lord" (Phil 2:9–11). Jesus rejected the false honour this world offered, and instead received the true honour that can only be given by the rightful ruler of creation, God himself.

7

God and Authority

God's Authority in Ancient Israel

Naboth treasured his vineyard. He loved resting out there in the cool of the evening after a day of pruning and weeding. His father had tended these vines, and his father before him. The whole land of Israel belonged to God, but this little patch of earth was God's special trust to Naboth and his family. God had entrusted this vineyard to them, to care for it and cultivate it as faithful stewards. When Naboth spent time in his vineyard, enjoying the shade of the broad leaves, smelling the rich earth, and feeling the gnarled trunks of the vines, his heart overflowed with joy and thankfulness as he sensed the Lord's presence with him.[1]

One day, King Ahab paid Naboth a visit. Naboth was alarmed, because he had been distressed and disturbed by the way Ahab was allowing his Phoenician wife Jezebel to take Israel deeper and deeper into disgusting Baal worship. Baal was considered the great storm god and Baal worshippers believed that only he could provide the rain that the land needed to be fertile, and to bear another harvest. Every summer Baal would disappear into the underworld, and for months there would be no rain. The people would then coax Baal into reappearing with his thunderclouds by performing actual sex acts with temple prostitutes, as though this would persuade him to make the soil fertile again.

Naboth, however, worshipped the one true God, Yahweh, who gave rain because of his covenant faithfulness, and who did not need to be cajoled or manipulated into keeping his promises. Nevertheless, as a loyal subject Naboth approached his monarch with a bow.

"What would my lord have his servant do for him?"

---

1. 1 Kings 21 recounts the story of Naboth, and Elijah's condemnation of Ahab.

Ahab answered, "I was thinking I should enlarge the vegetable patch next to my palace. Your vineyard is right next door, so name your price and I'll buy it from you."

Naboth's heart sank. "My lord, I would do anything else for you, but this land means a lot to me. My family has looked after it for generations, ever since it was allotted to us when Israel conquered this country."

Ahab looked taken aback at this refusal. "Oh, if it is some land you want, then I can give you a much better vineyard somewhere else."

This was becoming awkward for Naboth. It was not easy to resist his king's request. "I am very sorry, my lord, and deeply regret this. It is not because of the vineyard's sentimental value, or because I want to accumulate land. Basically, this plot is not mine to sell. It was entrusted to my family by Yahweh when he distributed the land among the tribes of Israel. It belongs to him and not to me!"

Ahab went back to his palace seething. He was so upset that he went to bed and wouldn't even eat. When his wife Jezebel found out the reason for his depression she laughed at him. "Is this how you Israelites govern? We Baal worshippers know how to rule. I'll show you what a real king does."

The next day the elders of the town announced that there was going to be a fast and a solemn assembly in order to avert disaster by confessing and repenting of sin. Naboth was puzzled by this, but gratified when he was given a place of honour. He began to feel uneasy when two known scoundrels came in and were given the right to address the assembly. He was horrified when they accused him of being the sinner in their midst – "We heard him curse God and the king!" – and urged the community to get rid of him. His horror turned to mounting fear and panic when the elders and nobles joined in, friends and neighbours who knew him and should have spoken up in his defence. Naboth had been set-up. Without being given any opportunity to answer the allegations or call other witnesses, he was dragged outside the town. He saw that a pile of stones had already been gathered, and the mob was looking forward to the spectacle of a gory public execution.

The conflict between Ahab and Naboth reflects the difference between Baal and Yahweh. Baal – meaning "lord" – was the capricious and despotic lord over the other minor gods and humans. Jezebel's understanding of kingship was based on the way Baal behaved as "lord." On the other hand, Yahweh held rulers to account and limited their authority by retaining the position of ultimate king, with ultimate ownership of the land. So, for example, when David abused his authority by taking Uriah's wife and having Uriah murdered, he was subject to God's judgement and justice just like anyone else (2 Sam 16; 17).

Since God himself is the ultimate source of authority, our view of God will inevitably shape our view of authority. If God is seen as capricious, controlling or threatening, then those leading or ruling out of that understanding will also behave in a capricious, controlling or threatening manner. If the God we worship is viewed as loving and faithful, then leaders will exercise their authority in a similar way.

Setting oneself up as the source of authority is an act of idolatry. There is no accountability and power is exercised for one's own benefit. The exercise of authority becomes self-centred, and the people in submission are used to further the ruler's agenda. Since there is no higher authority they are only subject to their leader, and in a sense, they exist to serve his purposes. His rhetoric may be full of orthodox God-language, but his behaviour demonstrates his belief that authority flows from himself and is to be used for the purpose of exalting himself. Since the authority is his, he has to defend it by enforcing the submission of others, if necessary, even through violence or lies.

Absolute Monotheism

A. W. Tozer wrote, "What comes into our minds when we think about God is the most important thing about us."[2] He meant that our concept of God fundamentally affects our thinking and drives our behaviour. The subconscious image we have of God is even more powerful. Since God is the ultimate ruler of the universe, our image and understanding of him will profoundly affect the way we exercise leadership, as well as what we expect from our leaders.

One of the most common views of God is that he is one in an absolute sense. He has no parts and no partners; in essence, he is nothing but oneness. This is an ancient idea, that originated with the Greek philosopher Pythagoras, who postulated that God was a monad, meaning "singularity." Plato then adopted this theory, and so it had a widespread influence on philosophy; and it was developed further by the neo-Platonists and Gnostics. Leibnitz, one of

---

2. A. W. Tozer, *The Knowledge of the Holy* (New York: HarperCollins, 1978), 1.

the most influential figures in Western European thought, also thought of God as a "monad" or an indivisible unity.

But the idea of the absolute oneness of God is most commonly associated with Muslim theology. Muhammad, the prophet of Islam, launched his movement as a protest against the multiplicity of idols that the citizens of Mecca were worshipping, and so the oneness of God became the fundamental tenet of Islam. Every day Muslims recite the *shahada*, the creed that is one of the five pillars of their religion: "There is no god but God, and Muhammad is the apostle of God." The doctrine of the oneness of God, *tawhid*, is one of their most important doctrines, often posited in contradiction to the Christian doctrines of the sonship of Christ and the Trinity. Surah Al Ikhlas of the Qur'an warns:

> Say, He is Allah, the One!
> Allah, the eternally Besought of all!
> He begetteth not, nor was begotten,
> And there is none comparable to Him.[3]

The idea of God as a single, absolute, indivisible unity sounds logical and attractively simple. Yet, Arab philosophers actually had intense debates as they struggled to make sense of the attributes that describe God's nature and actions. The Qur'an has several verses extolling the beautiful names of God – for instance, "His are the most beautiful names"[4] – while the traditions contained in the Hadiths state the number and importance of these names – "Allah has ninety-nine names, i.e. one-hundred minus one, and whoever knows them will go to Paradise."[5] This has led to a rich devotional practice of memorizing, reciting and meditating on the ninety-nine names of God: The Beneficent, The Merciful, The Eternal Lord, The Most Sacred, and so on. But theologians had heated arguments about these descriptions of God's nature, what they were and how they actually related to God's essence.

Around two hundred years after the birth of Islam the Arab theologian Al Ash'ari wrestled with these questions, and his followers, the Ash'arites, became one of the dominant schools in orthodox Sunni Islam. Many were concerned that talking about God's eternal attributes before the creation of the world led to the danger of these attributes becoming another uncreated entity alongside God, which would violate his absolute oneness. If God is merciful, who did he have mercy on before the creation of the world? Was there another being

---

3. M. M. Pickthall, *The Meaning of the Glorious Qur'an* (Beltsville, MD: Amana Publications, 1996), Surah 112:1–4.

4. Pickthall, Surah Taha 20:8.

5. Sahih Al-Bukhari 50:894.

alongside him – which was unthinkable – or did he have mercy on his creation, which would then make the creation eternal with him? Al Ash'ari insisted that the Qur'an taught that these attributes of God were indeed present eternally, but to protect God's absolute and unique oneness he argued they did not stem from his nature, but from the action of his free will. "Thus the divine will became the dominant factor in all thought of Absolute Oneness."[6] The attributes of God do not originate in the nature of God, and so cannot reveal his essence to us. Palestinian Muslim scholar Ismail Al Faruqi writes, "The will of God is the nature of God, in so far as I can know anything about him. This is God's will and that is all we have. God does not reveal himself to anyone."[7]

All that we can know of God is his unfettered will, free to do as he pleases and untrammelled by the constraints of his nature or law. Sayyid Qutub, one of the founders of the Muslim brotherhood in Egypt, concurred: "The divine will is free of all limitations and restrictions, even those based on a promise from Allah, or a law of his. For his will is absolute beyond any promise or law."[8] The implication of this is that God can seem to act capriciously, in contravention of one of his attributes. The early Persian scholar Al Razi wrote, "It is possible according to our religion that God may send blasphemers to paradise, and the righteous and worshippers to fire, because ownership belongs to him and no one can stop him."[9] Samuel Zwemer, the great pioneer missionary to the Muslim world, concluded, "The idea of absolute sovereignty of ruthless omnipotence are at the basis. For the rest his character is impersonal – that of an infinite, eternal, vast monad."[10]

Since the God of absolute oneness does not reveal himself, there is no possibility of relationship in the sense of knowing him. All that we can know is his absolute will, which means that the only way to relate to God is in absolute, unquestioning submission. Indeed, the word "Islam" means submission. Tozer said the most important thing about us is how we think about God, because our view of God shapes our view of the whole of life. Since the Muslim view of God emphasizes our submission to his will, relationships in the Muslim world also emphasize submission to authority.

---

6. Imad N. Shehadeh, *God With Us and Without Us, vol. 1* (Carlisle: Langham Global Library, 2018), 114. I am indebted to Dr Shehadeh for this material showing how Absolute Oneness of God leads to an exclusive focus on his will.

7. Isma'il Al-Faruqi, "On the Nature of Islamic Da'wah," *International Review of Mission* 65 (1976): 405.

8. Sayyid Qutub, *In the Shadow of the Qur'an* (Jeddah: Dar-al-'Elm, 1986), 6:30:3889.

9. Al-Razi, *The Commentary of Al-Razi* (Damascus: Dar-Al Fikr, 1981), 12:144.

10. Samuel M. Zwemer, *Moslem Doctrine of God* (New York: American Tract Society, 1905), 30.

In the time of Muhammad his followers expressed their loyalty to him by swearing allegiance and submission to him. In AD 628, he took 1,400 of his followers from Medina to Mecca to perform a pilgrimage at the Kaaba. The people of Mecca were understandably nervous and refused to allow them to enter the city. Muhammad sent his companion Uthman to negotiate terms for entry with the Meccans, and when he did not return on time it looked as if he had been killed. Faced with this opposition and possible conflict, Muhammad called his followers to pledge allegiance to him. This pledge took place under a tree and so was known as the Pledge of the Tree. During the pledging, each follower came before Muhammad and placed his hand on top of Muhammad's.

The Arabic for pledge or oath of allegiance is *bay'ah*. Etymologically, this is linked to the word for "sell." The idea is of selling or giving oneself to the leader in exchange for his guidance or protection. This event is referred to in the Qur'an, where God addresses Muhammad and says, "Allah was pleased with believers when they pledged allegiance to you."[11] The explanation given is that "those who pledge allegiance to you are actually pledging allegiance to Allah. The hand of Allah is over their hands."[12] As the followers placed their hands on Muhammad's they were also pledging allegiance to Allah, as submission to Muhammad becomes a way of expressing submission to God. The idea of submission to a spiritual leader being part of submission to God has continued in Islam to this day. In the Ahmadiyya movement new converts join the movement by expressing allegiance to their leader – or Caliph – in a ceremony of *bay'ah*, by laying their hands on that of their leader. The oath of allegiance has ten clauses, the last of which is obedience to the Caliph "in everything good, for the sake of Allah."

The more orthodox mystical Muslim movement of the Naqshbandis also initiates new members through a ceremony of *bay'ah*. Their website explains: "The seeker must follow a perfect Master able to guide him to the way of Allah, Almighty and Exalted, and to illuminate for him that way until he reaches the State of Annihilation. The seeker must give his oath and his promise to his guide, to learn from him how to leave his bad manners and to lift himself to better conduct in order to reach the Perfect Knowledge of Spirituality."[13] The path to illumination is through an oath of obedience to the perfect master. To follow the master is to follow God; to please the master is to please God; to disobey the master is to disobey God.

---

11. Pickthall, *The Meaning of the Glorious Qur'an,* Al Fath 48:18.

12. Pickthall, Al Fath 48:10.

13. http://naqshbandi.org/teachings/topics/taking-initiation-bayah/.

This does not only happen in religious orders but in the whole of society. In Islam, there is no distinction between sacred and secular, or between religious and political, so obedience to a political leader becomes a religious duty, and social or political leaders demand the same kind of loyalty that a spiritual leader expects. A recent example is president Tayyip Erdoğan of Turkey. In his book *Big Boss*, Mustafa Hoş – a well-known Turkish journalist – narrates how Erdoğan started life in a poor neighbourhood in Istanbul and rose to his current position of dominance and supremacy. He describes how Erdoğan requires his people to give him *biat*, which is the Turkish form of *bay'ah*. In one story, he recounts how businessman İnan Kıraç – son-in-law of Turkey's richest industrialist Vehbi Koç – was humiliated by Erdoğan. Kıraç was accustomed to being awarded lucrative government contracts. In the 2011 elections, he made the "mistake" of supporting the Republican People's Party (CHP) opposition and the contracts dried up. Kıraç went to Erdoğan to apologize. He was humiliated by being kept outside in a waiting room for ninety minutes, and then ushered in for a very brief, curt interview. A member of parliament commented that prominent businessmen must give their *biat* if they want government business, meaning that they must swear personal loyalty to Erdoğan to benefit from his gracious favours; if they show disloyalty, they should expect to be shamed and punished. The government is now regarded as Erdoğan's personal domain, and he understands his authority in the same absolute and personal terms as a religious leader.[14]

In 2015, Mustafa Hoş was arrested and faced trial for insulting the president. In June 2016 he was sentenced to fourteen months in prison, and ordered to pay a fine of $3,624.

Of course, there are many examples of bullying and controlling uses of authority outside the Muslim world, too; and there have been many Western leaders guilty of intimidation and violent repression. The lust for power afflicts rulers everywhere, causing them to lie and fight to gain it and keep it. It becomes so central to their identity that they cannot live without it. Indeed, there are many cases of husbands who call themselves Christian, but beat their wives. Their view of God is that of a harsh and distant tyrant, who threatens and punishes to enforce his will, and so they take it on themselves to emulate their God by forcing their wives into submission. Their sub-Christian concept of God results in sub-Christian treatment of their wives.

However, social scientists have found that societies around the world have different views of power and authority, and that some have a higher "power

---

14. Mustafa Hoş, *Big Boss* (Istanbul: Destek Yayınları, 2014).

distance" than others.[15] This means that authority figures are more remote, they are given more respect, and enjoy greater privileges. Leaders in such societies are not necessarily more abusive or domineering, as that depends on their attitude and understanding of their authority. My contention is that because of Islam's belief in Allah as being absolutely one, Muslim societies are more likely to suffer from overbearing leaders who see themselves as being above the law, and who are willing to use any and all means to hang on to their position and privileges.

Trinitarian Monotheism

The first Christian theologian to seriously face the challenge posed by Islam was St. John of Damascus. He hailed from a prestigious family, as his grandfather Mansour had been one of the city leaders who negotiated the terms of surrender to the Muslims in AD 635. His father Sergius was treasurer at the court of the Caliph of Damascus, and it seems that the well-educated John followed his father into government service at the highest levels. He was fluent in Greek and Arabic, and skilled in all the sciences of the day.

The details of John's life are sketchy and somewhat confused. He was born around AD 675, but even the date of his death is not certain. After some years of serving the Caliph, he resigned and joined the monastery of Saint Saba near Jerusalem. One reason given for this move is that the court was being gradually Islamicized. Another more exotic and entertaining account is that Leo III, the Byzantine emperor in Constantinople, was upset with John for defending the use of icons, and wrote a scurrilous letter to the Caliph accusing John of treachery. The angry Caliph had John's hand cut off, but John took the severed hand and prayed before an icon of Mary, and when he woke up in the morning it was miraculously restored! Seeing this, the Caliph apologized and offered to reinstate him, but John was now determined to devote the rest of his life to God.

After joining the monastery, John enjoyed the most fruitful period of his life, becoming a prolific writer of hymns, liturgy and theology. As he joined the great theological debates of his time, it is clear that he was influenced by his experience of having served in a Muslim court and having had discussions with Muslim clerics. He wrote scornfully against Islam as the "Heresy of the Ishmaelites" – because Muslims claim that the son Abraham took up the

---

15. Geert and Gert Jan Hofstede, and Michael Minkov, *Cultures and Organizations* (New York: McGraw Hill, 2010), 41.

mountain to sacrifice was Ishmael, and that the well of water God miraculously provided for Hagar and Ishmael is the Zam Zam well in Mecca today.

John of Damascus is most appreciated for his contribution towards the development of the doctrine of the Trinity. To Muslims, the concept of the Trinity is indefensible, as they understand it to mean tritheism – that there are three gods. The Qur'an even suggests that the Trinity consists of the Father, the Son and Mother Mary! John reached back to the work of the Cappadocian Fathers who had first got to grips with the doctrine of the Trinity. They were writing after the Arian heresy against Christ's deity had been defeated at the Council of Nicea in AD 325, and the discussion had moved on to the nature of the Holy Spirit. Basil of Caesarea showed that the Spirit shared the same divine essence as the Father and the Son. Each person of the Godhead is involved in everything that God does: in creation, in our redemption through Christ's death, and in the final judgement. What then is the relationship between the Father, the Son and the Spirit? Gregory of Nyssa insisted that they were distinct entities, not to be thought of as the same as each other. The biblical language was that the Son was generated or begotten by the Father, whereas the Spirit proceeded from the Father and the Son. Gregory of Nazianzus went further in defending the deity of the Holy Spirit, arguing that if the Spirit is not God, then we cannot be sanctified or become "participants of the divine nature" (2 Pet 1:4).

Faced with the challenge of the claim that God is one in an absolute sense, John had to show how God's triune nature could not be understood to mean that God is three. He took the concept of *perichōrēsis*, first used by Gregory of Nazianzus, to describe the mutual indwelling of the three – the Father abides in the Son and in the Holy Spirit, and likewise the Son abides in the Father and in the Spirit. *Perichōrēsis* derives from *chōra*, "which means 'space' or 'room' and is the nominal form of the verb *chōreō*, 'to make room for'; plus the preposition peri, which means 'around' or 'about.' But it came to be used to express how one person can be open to another."[16] It therefore describes how people share with and include one another. John of Damascus developed the *perichōrēsis* by combining it with the idea of coinherence, that the three exist through a mutual exchange of life, that they find their being in each other and cannot exist in isolation. They are open to each other to such an extent that they share their very selves. Their unity is in the intensity of their relationships with each

---

16. Dennis F. Kinlaw, *Let's Start with Jesus: A New Way of Doing Theology* (Grand Rapids: Zondervan, 2005), 82.

other, as they live in and through each other. They are three, but such is the intensity of mutual self-giving that they are indeed one.

Imad Shehadeh has shown how a Trinitarian view of God's oneness can resolve the Arab philosophers' struggles with the problem of his attributes. If God's essential nature is love, then he must always have been loving, and must always have had an object of his love, with love between him and the beloved. If God is absolutely one there is no possibility of his having had anyone to love before the creation of the universe, but if there is a plurality within the one Godhead then there can also be love between the Father and the Son, mediated by the Holy Spirit. The love between the persons of the Trinity secures the attribute of love as an essential aspect of his nature. Shehadeh writes, "Every attribute requires a relationship, and the presence of a relationship assures the protection of each attribute."[17]

The eleventh-century French spiritual leader Bernard of Clairvaux commented on the Song of Songs in this boldly poetic way: "If, as is properly understood, the Father is he who kisses, the Son he who is kissed, then it cannot be wrong to see in the kiss the Holy Spirit, for he is the imperturbable peace of the Father and the Son, their unshakable bond, their undivided love, their indivisible unity."[18] As we then come to the Father through the Son, we too are kissed by the Spirit as he assures us of God's love for us! Shehadeh rightly comments that the Trinity is not to be seen as an embarrassing problem to be solved, but "a beauty to be continually discovered and enjoyed."[19]

Similarly, early Muslim theologians struggled with the question whether the Qur'an was created or not. The Qur'an and the Hadiths themselves indicate that the Qur'an was eternally present with God as his word, but that invited the logical objection that the Qur'an was another eternal entity with God, implying the very serious sin of *shirk*, or ascribing a partner to God. The conflict grew so heated that, for a time, the Abbasid Caliph Al Ma'mun persecuted those who held that the Qur'an was uncreated. A Trinitarian view of God resolves this tension by holding forth the Son as the uncreated Word of God, eternally with the Father and uniquely able to reveal the Father's nature to mankind. The Trinity provides the grounds for the one God to reveal his true, unchanging self, and to invite us to participate in a loving relationship with him.

---

17. Shehadeh, *God With Us and Without Us*, 136.

18. St. Bernard of Clairvaux, *Sermons on the Song of Songs* (USA: Beloved Publishing, 2014), 34.

19. Shehadeh, *God With Us and Without Us*, 149.

The Trinity and Authority

In the twentieth century Jürgen Moltmann[20] went back to the Trinity and to John's idea of *perichōrēsis*, and demonstrated its significance for how we view leadership and authority. Moltmann was German. Having experienced the disastrous consequences of Hitler's leadership in the Second World War, he was deeply concerned about the damage done by totalitarian rulers who pride themselves on their strength and authority. He understood that the early church had emphasized the oneness of God in the face of the idolatry of the ancient world, but saw a danger in overemphasizing the oneness of God, or the dominance of the Father eclipsing the Son and the Holy Spirit. He argued that this monism – believing in the absolute and undifferentiated oneness of God – led to distorted ideas of authority. It suggests that the one in authority should be self-sufficient, aloof from those under him, making decisions by himself, and coercing others to obey. He saw this leadership style replicated in dictators who lorded it over their subjects, and in church leaders for whom spiritual leadership was about exalting themselves and building their own reputations.

For Moltmann, the *perichōrēsis* of John of Damascus was a most welcome correction. God himself was not a cold, remote, abstract concept, but essentially relational. Likewise, the Father was not a stern disciplinarian, dominating the Son and the Spirit, but in deep, open and reciprocal relationship with them. God is love, and this love is primarily and originally lived out in community. The Father loves the Son and the Son loves the Father. The Father abides in the Son and the Son abides in the Father. The Father glorifies the Son and the Son glorifies the Father. The Spirit is the third, sharing these relationships, yet in a different way, sent by the Father and revealing the Son. The Father's aim is not to glorify himself, but that all creation should give glory to the Son. He is not jealous of the Son when he is worshipped, but rejoices in the exaltation of his Son. He does not accomplish this alone, but with and through the action of the Holy Spirit. In doing so the Father is truly a father, and lives out fatherhood for us. In sending, empowering, indwelling and glorifying the Son, the Father is showing us the essence of fatherhood.

Moltmann and his disciple Miroslav Volf hold these Trinitarian relationships up as a model for leadership. Godly leadership is not the preserve of strong individuals who create and dominate organizations to fulfil their vision; rather, the Trinity shows us that true leadership happens in relational communities, where individuals come together in profound sharing and

---

20. Jurgen Moltmann, *The Trinity and the Kingdom* (Minneapolis: Fortress Press, 1993), 176, 197–202.

mutual submission. Their lives are interconnected through love, they rejoice in one another's victories, they use their gifts and abilities to serve one another.

Viv Thomas has developed the thinking of Moltmann and Volf to reflect on how this Trinitarian model of leadership should affect organizations.[21] God himself is essentially relational, so effective leadership and leadership teams are chiefly characterized by healthy relationships. Effective teams foster creativity, which flourishes when there is an atmosphere of trust and acceptance, encouraging members to be open with one another in sharing new ideas. Effective leaders understand that they can only fully accomplish God's mission through others, which means they are committed to empowering and developing those around them. Teams perform well when the members are able to complement one another by exercising their diverse abilities and talents. As the Father, the Son and the Holy Spirit differ from one another in the variety of their roles, leadership fosters diversity and welcomes different perspectives. Wise leaders know that they need people who can constructively disagree with them.

Godly Leadership

To summarize this chapter, what we believe about God fundamentally shapes the way we lead. The belief that God is absolutely one, with no partner or associate, leads to the idea that he imposes his will on the universe through power and intimidation. This results in leaders who think they should dominate, expect absolute personal loyalty, and punish any questioning or independence on the part of those under them. Of course, this model of leadership has existed since the beginning of history, and this Muslim view of leadership reflects the values of the Arab culture where it originated. Many other cultures around the world also subscribe to this view of authority, where strong individuals cannot brook any dissent or threat to their pre-eminence. At the same time, Islam has greatly influenced the cultures where it is practised, encouraging leaders to dominate and control to defend their position and honour. One consequence of this is that no Muslim nation has been able to sustain a viable democracy. Turkey was the welcome exception to this rule; but in 2018 we witnessed how Erdoğan's drive towards Islamicization led to the rewriting of the constitution to ensure that, as president, all power is in his hands. Parliament has been reduced to a rubber stamp, and the judges are all his appointees. The result is prisons full of anyone who dares to criticize or question him.

---

21. Viv Thomas, "Leading with Trinity" (PhD Thesis, University of London, 2002).

Serving under a Muslim ruler, John of Damascus was the first Christian theologian to engage with the claims of absolute monotheism, and it is not a coincidence that his greatest theological contribution was to take our understanding of the Trinity further than anyone else up to that time. His vision of God was radically different from Muslim thought, for the Father shared his nature with the Son and the Spirit, giving himself to them, living with them in the deepest and most intimate communion, and together with them putting into action a plan of salvation that would result in the Son enjoying the honour and pre-eminence of being "the firstborn within a large family" (John 8:29). This is the model of leadership we must embrace. It will not be easy, because our fallen natures always seek to enthrone self and our fallen cultures profoundly shape our values. The pursuit of honour is deeply engrained in our hearts and minds, and we see the bitter fruit of this in dysfunction and chaos in organizations and societies all around the world today.

There is a better way, modelled for us by Jesus. In the next chapter I explore what this looks like.

8

Leadership Redeemed

Leadership Lessons

We now consider how this Trinitarian understanding of leadership works out in practice. How do godly patrons behave towards their clients, and how do leaders who are not concerned about their own honour treat their followers? We look to the example of Jesus, especially the way he dealt with his disciples on their last evening together. As he prepared them for his imminent death, he continued to lead them as he had always done, for "he loved them to the end" (John 13:1). However, he was also thinking beyond the immediate crisis to the challenge of handing over leadership of his movement to this group of men who were still arguing about who was the greatest, and who should have the pre-eminent positions when Jesus finally established his kingdom. The Upper Room discourse (John 13–17) reveals several key traits of Jesus that all leaders must emulate.

Attitudes of godly leaders

1.   Personal care and attention
Jesus "got up from the table, took off his outer robe, and tied a towel around himself" (John 13:4). The main reason Jesus washed his disciples' feet was to set an example of how they too should serve one another. However, his actions also give us a picture of what that service should look like, for he was attentive to the obvious fact that they were about to sit down to eat with dirty feet – no small concern when we remember that they were "reclining at table," so their feet were not hidden and out of the way under the table! Jesus was aware of their personal needs. His actions were deeply humiliating, since washing the guests' feet was a task reserved for the lowest servant in the house, usually a

gentile slave. Moreover, feet themselves were considered especially dirty and shameful – as they still are today in many parts of the Middle East and Asia. In touching their feet, Jesus was touching a sensitive and intimate part of their bodies – embarrassing for them and demeaning for him, but at the same time, creating a special sense of personal connection. If the person touching their feet was a mere slave, they could have ignored it as being of no consequence; but when it was Jesus touching them in this way there would have been a feeling of intense closeness.

Many leaders want to avoid such personal closeness and rapport with their followers, because they think they must maintain a distance in order to protect their authority. They fear that closeness will lead to a loss of respect. Members of an Indian Christian organization told me how remote their leader seemed, because he remained distant and his gatekeepers made it difficult to approach him. On the other hand, an American director of a humanitarian development organization in Yemen told me about an incident during the early days of the civil war. Worried because one of the staff was very late to work one day, he asked the others if they knew what had happened. When the worker eventually turned up the director was quick to ask if he was all right. He overheard other staff members remark, "See how much he cares about us!" They were surprised because they were used to bosses who seldom expressed concern and whose main reaction would have been to rebuke the latecomer with a warning not to do it again.

2.   Desire to see followers excel

Javad, an Iranian friend, came to me excited after reading about Jesus's aspirations for his disciples and the promise that they would do even "greater works" than he had done (John 14:12). Javad was astonished that a great leader like Jesus would want his disciples to excel in this way. He had been used to leaders who were anxious to make sure their followers could not surpass them and become a potential threat to their position. He was familiar with leaders who wanted followers to advance to the point where they could be useful helpers, but not to the point where they might eclipse the leader in importance.

In chapter 2 I recounted the well-known story of a great Persian wrestler and his apprentice. The wrestler made sure he remained greater than his apprentice by not teaching him one final, special move. Some years ago, I discussed this story with the Afghan staff of an NGO in Kabul. They immediately recognized the truth of the story, and one of them commented, "It's no wonder Afghanistan is going backwards and becoming poorer, when each successive generation has a little less knowledge than the one before!"

3.   Self-disclosure

The Upper Room discourse reveals another characteristic of Jesus's leadership – his openness and transparency with his disciples: "I have called you friends, because I have made known to you everything that I have heard from my Father" (John 15:15). We have already noted that many leaders boost their authority by appearing remote. Such leaders also understand that knowledge is power, and so withhold information in order to keep their followers dependent on them. While being able to keep confidences is an important quality of leaders – especially because they are often privy to sensitive information that should not be shared widely – clear and adequate communication is also vital, as it enables followers to understand the situation and make decisions for themselves. As Jesus was preparing to hand over leadership to the apostles it was important that they understood as much as they could of the Father's plan.

Jesus modelled personal openness, not only in passing on what he had heard from the Father, but also in living out his rich emotional life. His disciples were with him as he wept in sorrow, rebuked hypocrites in anger, and felt deep compassion for the broken people all around him. For us – unlike Jesus, who was sinless – personal openness will also mean not hiding our weaknesses and failures. Many leaders are afraid of admitting ignorance or mistakes because they think this will diminish their standing. Actually, it often enhances their position in the eyes of their followers, presenting a more accurate model of the Christian life, since our discipleship does not depend on our perfect performance but on God's forgiveness and grace. Similarly, our authority does not stem from our perfect knowledge or behaviour, but from God's gift and calling.

George Verwer – founder of Operation Mobilization – shocked many in the 1960s by talking openly about his struggles with pornography, quite unlike other preachers who avoided such controversial topics. Rather than undermining his spiritual authority, this openness enhanced it, as many young people were attracted by his integrity and lack of religious hypocrisy. Many committed their lives to embracing Verwer's mission because his personal reality persuaded them that they could trust him.

4.   Humility

In chapter 4 we studied Paul's great hymn proclaiming Christ's humiliation and exaltation (Phil 2:6–11), and noted that his purpose in presenting this magnificent truth was to add strength to his exhortation to unity in the face of the honour-seeking social pressures driving the believers apart. Paul begins the chapter by referring to five key attitudes – two to be avoided and three to be encouraged – that are critical in the pursuit of harmony (Phil 2:3–4):

- "Selfish ambition" (*eritheia*): This word originally meant a day labourer; after Aristotle, it came to have connotations of a lowly person scheming and plotting to advance himself, which results in discord, factions and strife. It describes someone with sharp elbows, pushing rivals out of the way. The same word is used in Philippians 1:17 of Paul's rivals, who see his imprisonment as an opportunity to grab the limelight by preaching the gospel and adding to Paul's suffering in jail. This ugly, shameful attitude is the opposite of that of Jesus, who did not cling to equality with God, but rather let go of the glory and "emptied himself."

- "Conceit" (*kenodoxia*): The root is "empty glory," an inflated and unrealistic sense of one's own importance. Such people think they deserve greater honour and higher positions because they are better qualified than anyone else. When someone else is praised they are filled with jealousy and anger. Galatians 5:26 says conceited people are competitive and envious, probably looking for ways to put others down.

- "Humility" (*tapeinophrosune*): Although humility is often regarded as a positive trait in cultures influenced by Christianity, for the Greek philosophers of Paul's time it had negative connotations, conveying the idea of pettiness, obsequiousness, submissiveness. When Paul called the Philippian church – particularly the "bishops and deacons" addressed by the letter (Phil 1:1) – to live in humility, he was calling them to a radically countercultural rejection of the honour-seeking behaviour valued by their compatriots. He challenged them with the example of Christ (Phil 2:8), but if they had adopted this attitude their peers would have reacted first with incredulity, and then with sneering scorn.

- "Better than yourselves" (*huperecho*): This carries the idea of being more significant or of surpassing value. Romans saw life as a *cursus honorum*, or a race for honours, so this call to regard others as superior in honour, rank or power cut across the very foundation of contemporary culture. Romans 12:10 makes the same point: "Outdo one another [or take the lead] in showing honour." Sincerely and genuinely find ways to honour others, instead of seeking honour for oneself.

- "Look to the interests of others" (*skopeo*): This means taking care of others' interests, as well as my own, and considering how to advance their agendas; not competing with them or looking for ways to hinder their progress; becoming their servant rather than their rival. Christ took on the form of a slave in order to secure our salvation.

Instead of constantly fighting to gain status on the basis of a false estimation of their own importance, Paul calls the Philippian leaders to something unheard of – a humility that esteems others as superior to oneself, and which expresses itself practically by looking out for others' concerns. Paul exposes the emptiness of the old code of honour and calls the Philippians to a new code, in which God grants true and lasting honour to those who do the honourable thing of laying down their lives for others. Hellerman titled his monograph on this passage "Reconstructing Honor."[1]

Authority and respect

All this raises fundamental questions for leaders functioning in hierarchical cultures where people have been brought up to expect a leader to be domineering and distant. If leaders encourage personal closeness, talk about their weaknesses, and regard others as better than themselves, how then will they command the respect of their followers? If a teacher answers a student's question with, "What do you think?" or even "I don't know," will the class not start to get restive and rebellious?

I am not arguing that all leaders should adopt a Western democratic, consultative model of leadership. I am well aware that this approach is deeply rooted in Western culture, and that attempts to lead in this style in other parts of the world will be met by confusion, frustration and ultimately contempt. I remember an international missionary team where an Asian leader upset his Western team members by his authoritarian style – being very directive, barking orders and getting upset when he was questioned. Behind his back, they compared him to Hitler! His Western successor adopted the opposite style, going to great lengths to solicit everyone's opinion. But the Asian team members found this difficult to accept, complaining that the leader's job was to make decisions and that their new leader was weak and abdicating his responsibility to lead!

---

1. Joseph H. Hellerman, *Reconstructing Honor in Roman Philippi* (Cambridge: Cambridge University Press, 2009).

The Bible clearly teaches that authority is from God, and is an essential element of leadership. Despite Jesus's brilliant use of questions – helping people clarify their thinking and exposing the inconsistencies in their assumptions – he never sought the disciples' advice about what they should do next. It was Jesus who heard his Father's voice and understood the mission they were on, so he was the one who clearly and boldly gave directions. When there was grumbling or dissent, he did not hesitate to rebuke, sometimes in the harshest terms. Similarly, after all the boasts about his weakness, Paul closes the Corinthian correspondence with the wish that he would not "have to be severe in using the authority that the Lord has given me for building up and not for tearing down" (2 Cor 13:10).

Likewise, the glorious oneness and mutuality of the Trinity, with each person loving and glorifying the others, should not lead us to think that the Father is no longer the ultimate source of all authority. The Cappadocian fathers proved their point that the Son is not subordinate to the Father, in the sense he is as fully divine as the Father, and is to be worshipped along with the Father. Nevertheless, the Son always submitted to the Father, for he said, "I seek to do not my own will but the will of him who sent me" (John 5:30). Neither was his obedience limited to his time on earth, for from eternity he was always the Son, begotten by the Father, and therefore dependent on the Father; and as the perfect Son, always fully submissive to the Father. His perfect submission does not detract from his glory as a member of the Godhead, but makes him the perfect Word, fully revealing the Father's grace and truth.

Leaders must be confident of their authority, but not authoritarian; leading, but not lording over. This will be worked out differently in different cultures, but the key is knowing that the authority they exercise is from God and not from themselves. When leaders start believing that their authority is theirs on the basis of their gifts, power or virtue, then they have begun to commit idolatry. In effect, they have put themselves in the place of God. Since most Christian leaders would agree that their authority is from God, it is difficult to discern how a leader truly understands his authority. Since we are human, and prone to self-deception, our motives are inevitably mixed, for we are not fully aware of the deep-seated beliefs that drive our behaviour. However, here are two tests to aid discernment:

First, since their authority is from God, godly leaders do not need to defend it. Like Jesus and Paul, they are able to assume the role of a servant in the assurance that God will defend and validate their authority. They do not need to show off their authority or fight to impose it or put down those who criticize them; rather, they are aware that if they assert their own authority they are in danger of corrupting it.

Second, since their authority is from God, they use it for the benefit of others. This is the true meaning of servant leadership, which is sometimes misunderstood to mean weakly complying with the wishes of others. True leaders do not use their God-given authority to make their own lives comfortable, garnish their reputations or accumulate wealth; instead, they use it to advance the welfare of those in their care, often even at their own expense.

Church Planting Movements

This understanding of leadership is essential to see movements of churches. If our goal is the evangelization of non-Christian societies, the only way church growth can keep up with and exceed population growth is through exponential multiplication, in which churches reproduce to form churches, which then in turn reproduce to produce third-, fourth- and fifth-generation churches. Gifted leaders are able to gather people around themselves so that a congregation grows. But such growth reaches a plateau – usually determined by the level of the leader's capacity and talents. Simply bringing people into the church, to enjoy the preaching and worship, cannot result in the rapid growth which the apostles saw in the first century, and which we need to see today. Instead of mere addition to the congregation, we need multiplication of congregations. This can only happen if believers are sent out into the community, empowered to actively form groups themselves. Developing, training and releasing new leaders is vital for this process.

I was recently involved in training church planters to start new groups using the "Discovery Bible Study" tool, which was developed by David Watson in India as part of his "Disciple Making Movements." This method consists of a simple inductive Bible study, in which group members read a passage together several times, and then share how it spoke to them and how they are going to apply this truth during the week ahead. In just a few weeks, people can learn how to run these groups, and then start their own groups with their friends or relatives. Two gifted and enthusiastic individuals went back to their home towns after the training and quickly formed new groups. However, these groups never multiplied. Whenever the leaders I had trained went off on a trip they cancelled the next meeting, because they did not believe anyone in the group could provide adequate leadership; as a result, they never developed leaders to start new groups. They thought the success of the meeting depended on their presence, and that without them the group could not manage. They were enjoying the experience of leading the group, and did not want anyone else to take that from them. Raising up the next generation of leaders means handing over both our privileges and responsibilities, allowing others to take our place, and then releasing them to flourish on their own.

A veteran church planter from Indonesia – who has overseen a movement that has grown to 18,000 groups in twenty years – shared with us that an important key was to "reconfigure honour." He realized that the natural instinct of his church planters was to keep adding members to their house churches, as more members made them feel more important and more successful. To counter this, he would organize celebrations every time a church planter reported the formation of a new group, with all the other church planters clapping, cheering and congratulating their colleague who had managed to raise up and release a new leader. In this way the church planters learnt that true, godly honour came from giving away status and position, not gaining a larger and larger gathering of followers.

A colleague in the Near East has told me that another dimension of working towards church planting movements is working with pluralistic leadership teams. Many of the people he is training come from the traditional churches, where they are frustrated with the typical patron pastor who keeps everything under his control, so growth can only go as far as that one man has energy and ability to sustain the organization. They see the need for a different style of leadership, where there is shared decision-making and effective delegation. The traditional pastors are willing to allow innovative approaches to evangelism among Muslims through forming new groups, but then expect all the new believers to attend their worship services, even though they find the structure and format alien and off-putting. The desire to maximize the number of people sitting in the church on a Sunday morning takes precedence over the needs of new believers for congenial groups where they feel accepted and can flourish.

Westerners and Submission

The challenge for Westerners is somewhat different. When we read scriptural exhortations to "obey your leaders and submit to them" (Heb 13:17) our first reaction is often to raise objections, to blunt the force of the command with limitations and exceptions. Postmodern thinking has taught us to be suspicious of all authority, to view authority in and of itself as inherently corrupt and used to coerce in order to impose the selfish agenda of the ruler. Sadly, recent instances of misusing spiritual authority in the church to justify abuse, and then to protect the perpetrators, has only added to this suspicion. Authority may ultimately be from God, but he has delegated it to flawed, human vessels, who twist and debase it for their own purposes.

Nevertheless, our submission to God's authority is often expressed in submission to human authorities. Submission is an ancient spiritual discipline that teaches us to trust when we do not understand and requires us to face up to our rebellious natures. There is something in all of us that rankles when we are ordered to do something, and we need to recognize that reaction as sinful and stand against it. We need to recover the joy of wholehearted submission. Working under a leader from another culture is often a wonderful opportunity to learn about obeying without objecting or demanding an explanation, delighting in offering loyal service.

I first went to India with OM at the age of twenty-two, one year after my conversion from a typical 1960s background as a student protester. In 1969, during my first year at Manchester University, I had gleefully joined a group that were occupying the administration block, demanding that the authorities disclose any "secret files" they held. Our "sit in" lasted a week, with local rock bands giving free concerts amid clouds of marijuana smoke. It now seems quite reasonable to me that the university should have the right to hold confidential information; but back then the excitement of the Vietnam war protests in the USA and the student riots in Paris made us determined to oppose authority at every opportunity.

I arrived in India in 1974, just twenty-seven years after India had gained independence from the British empire. As a white Englishman, I was greeted with deference by some Indians – who were grateful for the positive aspects of colonial government – and resentment from others – who remembered the injustice and violence used to suppress the independence movement. It would have been easy enough for me to adopt an unconscious attitude of superiority or to feel a sense of entitlement to rule. After my initial experience under the firm and disciplined leadership of S. N. Das and Resham Raj, I was sent to Orissa to serve under Dhananjaya Nayak. Although there were times I was tempted to criticize his approach, I soon realized that my responsibility was to loyally serve him. I could have made life difficult for him by second-guessing his decisions, but I knew that my role was to help him do well. Instead of encouraging complaints about his work ethic from other team members, I stood up for him, and went to him privately if it became necessary to raise an issue. The fruitfulness of our mission, which depended on Nayak's success, would have been badly undermined if I had tried to showcase my talents at his expense. Instead, learning to cheerfully do as I was told, without questioning or grumbling, was a crucial part of my spiritual formation and cross-cultural training, teaching me the value of respect and obedience.

This kind of joyful submission should not be confused with silence in the face of abuse or injustice. As children of light we are called to speak truth, and when we see authority being misused we should and must voice our concerns. We should, however, do so while continuing to respect the authority placed over us, not venting personal anger, and with an attitude of seeking our leaders' best and trying to help them succeed. Similarly, the church must be careful not to lose its prophetic voice in society. Being "subject to the governing authorities" (Rom 13:1) does not mean we should not speak out against injustice. The failure of many Bible-believing Christians to protest against Apartheid in South Africa and Jim Crow policies in the southern states of the United States has seriously undermined our credibility today; those who spoke up peacefully, with dignity and respect – like Bishop Desmond Tutu and Dr Martin Luther King Jr – were welcome exceptions who are an example to us today.

Westerners working in Asia or Africa often feel embarrassed when they are honoured with public displays of deference. They cringe when given seats in the front of the church, when people offer to carry their briefcases, or when formal speeches extol their achievements. We have become so egalitarian, valuing informality so highly, that this kind of behaviour seems slightly absurd. Sometimes Western Christians react against this by refusing to accept the honour, thinking that by so doing they are modelling servant leadership – but all they achieve is to cause confusion and even give offence. The story is told of an British principal of a theological seminary in West Africa. Wanting to teach a lesson in servanthood, he began to do the gardener's work of cutting the grass in the seminary garden. This caused great consternation among his staff. They remonstrated with him, explaining that his behaviour was causing them intense embarrassment. The sight of the principal of a respected institution doing the work of a gardener was bringing shame on the whole institution, and outsiders were mocking the principal's inability to get his own staff to do their jobs properly. His actions did not appear commendable to them, but bizarre. Perhaps he could have better served them by conforming to their expectations, and humbled himself by accepting their norms.

Why then was Jesus washing his disciples' feet so stunningly effective? How do we follow his example? Part of the answer is that Jesus, as an insider to the culture, was able to accurately gauge how his action would be perceived and what influence it would have. The timing was also significant, as the setting of the Passover and the sense of a looming crisis added great poignancy to a simple act. This symbolic action also had a profound influence because it was the exception to the norm, since the foot washing was typically carried out by a slave. By washing the disciples' feet Jesus was neither denying his authority nor pretending to be on the same level as them, for in explaining his actions he said, "You call me Teacher and Lord – and you are right, for that is what I am" (John 13:13).

The Trinitarian model also challenges the way the Western church has allowed corporate thinking to affect its leadership. While there are profound insights to be gained from the wisdom of secular writers like Peter Drucker and Patrick Lencioni, too often success is defined by numbers, budgets and buildings; and growth is understood in terms of mechanistic programmes that leave little room for the work of the Spirit. Pastors see themselves as CEOs of companies, driving their congregations to achieve their personal vision statements and finding their own significance in the adulation of their members. This individualism does not allow for the teams of leaders to practice loving and submitting to each other as we see in the New Testament. Rather, like honour-driven patron leaders, they feed on their success until, with time, they become so puffed up that they consider themselves above accountability, resulting in an inevitable fall, accompanied by scandal and disgrace.

Suffering and Enemies

Leaders who want to exert an influence in the kingdom of God by following the example of Jesus and Paul must be ready to pay the price of personal suffering. As they choose to flout the expectations of their cultures they will be met with misunderstanding, scorn and hostility. Australian scholar Peter Marshall has described the fiercely antagonistic honour system in the ancient Greek and Romans worlds, where people gained social status by doing good to their friends or harm to their enemies. Enmity could be caused by jealousy, rivalry or disappointment and he quotes an old Greek proverb, "Help your friends and harm your enemies." They pushed themselves up by pushing others down, gaining honour at the expense of others. Often, this was by using their powers of rhetoric to mock or shame their enemies with biting invective.[2] Isak Lund has shown that even Cicero, the famous Roman orator, was not above using fabricated sexual allegations to destroy an opponent's reputation.[3] This could

---

2. Peter Marshall, *Enmity in Corinth: Social Conventions in Paul's Relations with the Corinthians* (Tubingen: Mohr Siebeck, 1987), 48, 52.

3. Isak Lund, *Making Enemies: The Logic of Immorality in Ciceronian Oratory* (Lund: Lund University), 52–70.

then lead to destroying the enemy's social circle by getting his friends to shun him. The ultimate weapon was to humiliate them by defeating them on the battlefield or in the law courts.

Paul was attacked in all these ways in his struggles with the churches in Galatia (Gal 4:16) and Corinth (2 Cor 10:10). Leaders who strive to live for righteousness in shame-honour cultures today will suffer the same fate. King David also had many enemies, and the book of Psalms has an astonishing 120 verses which speak of this enmity. When he became the target of malicious gossip that fabricated lies to ruin his good reputation David wrote, "They make their tongue sharp as a snake's, and under their lips is the venom of vipers" (Ps 140:3). The most hurtful attack is when a close friend becomes an enemy in an act of betrayal. David wrote, "Even my bosom friend in whom I trusted, who ate of my bread, has lifted the heel against me" (Ps 40:9).

We are often taken aback at the violence of the psalmist's prayers against his enemies, and struggle to know how to apply these to our circumstances today. One interpretative key is to read them through the lens of Christ, who fulfilled all these verses in his own life when he "endured such hostility against himself from sinners" (Heb 12:3). It was Jesus who took the widely-accepted saying of his own day, "You shall love your neighbour and hate your enemy" (Matt 5:43), and turned it into a command so radical that no one else dared teach it: "Love your enemies and pray for those who persecute you" (Matt 5:44). Jesus suffered mocking, false accusations and betrayal as his enemies sought to humiliate and destroy him; yet, at the very end, we find him praying, "Father, forgive them" (Luke 23:34). Christian leaders who follow his example today will suffer the same hostility, but will also share his glorious vindication. After his resurrection, Jesus ascended into heaven, sat down at the right hand of his Father, and was told to wait until his enemies became his footstool. Either in this life or the next, we too will be exalted by the one who is able to bestow the highest honours imaginable.

Epilogue

A Waterfall of Troubles

Hormoz Shariat,[1] like many others, fled the chaos of the Islamic regime in Iran; he settled in California, where he gained a PhD and became a successful research scientist. Around the same time, he became a Christian, and a group of friends began meeting in his home for prayer and Bible study. The group grew, and they asked Hormoz to be their pastor. Despite some misgivings he accepted this invitation. For ten years, the church enjoyed success, growing steadily until it had around 120 members. Then one of the elders started opposing Hormoz, accusing him of not having a calling or an anointing, and not being gifted as a pastor. Hormoz was aware that his primary gifting was more apostolic than pastoral, but still felt that he was called to serve that church. The elder recruited some friends, who went around the homes of church members slandering Hormoz and campaigning for his removal. Some of his friends wanted Hormoz to respond to the charges against him, but he refused to defend himself. All this opposition made him feel so discouraged that he considered going back to his old job as a scientist. Then he had a vision of himself standing underneath a waterfall, with the Lord saying, "This is a waterfall of troubles, stand under it, do not run away."

The campaign against Hormoz gathered pace. Finally, a church meeting was called, at which the members voted to remove him from being pastor. When the opposition won this vote of no confidence they went out to celebrate, and Hormoz sensed the Lord saying, "Go and celebrate with them!" They all went to a restaurant. Hormoz ordered a hamburger, which came with a "happy flag" stuck in the bun. When Hormoz saw the flag he felt the joy of the Lord, and sensed him saying, "You think this is the worst day of your life, but it is the best!" To this day, he has kept the flag to remember that moment when the intense pain of his disgrace was turned to joy.

Despite the humiliation Hormoz had suffered, he asked to remain as a member of the church, and used to sit quietly at the back of the church. The elders who had taken over the church were struggling with the preaching, and surprisingly, asked Hormoz to resume his pulpit ministry. Despite this, the

---

1. Rev Dr Hormoz Shariat related these events to me when I met him personally.

animosity and hatred continued, with the attacks growing more vicious: "You have demons, someone had a vision of you with a snake in your belly." Hormoz went to church prayer meetings, where a lot of the prayers were horizontal messages aimed at him. All this caused him a great deal of heartache. When he prayed for healing for his heart, he found he was filled with a supernatural love for his persecutors, able to look at them and pray for them with genuine compassion. During these days he often enjoyed sweet fellowship with the Lord, sensing the nearness of his amazing presence.

A significant minority of the church still supported Hormoz. They called in a mediator, who eventually recommended that the two parties go their separate ways – and so the church split. Hormoz was left with a remnant of discouraged people. But then God stepped in with an extraordinary explosion of life and love. In just a couple of years, their numbers grew from 50 to 250. Hormoz recalls, "Anyone who came into the church was saved." This period of supernatural health came because the members were "sick of division, pride and gossip." The church multiplied from one congregation to six, and they started a television ministry which has gone on to flourish and prosper, with many house churches springing up in Iran in response to their message.

This true story illustrates the main message of this book. Hormoz went through dark days of shame and disgrace, the victim of venomous personal attacks. God gave him the grace not to retaliate or walk away, but to endure and to keep loving. He found grace to endure the humiliation, as he accepted God's call to give up the purple. Eventually he was vindicated, with a greatly increased ministry that reached thousands of Iranians – not only in California but even in Iran itself. He was willing to accept the loss of his own reputation, and in return God rewarded him with a wider ministry and international prominence.

The Grand Inquisitor

In his great novel *The Brothers Karamazov* the Russian novelist Fyodor Dostoyevsky has the unbelieving Ivan Karamazov tell the "Legend of the Grand Inquisitor" to his believing brother Aloysha. In this legend, Jesus comes to Seville during the Spanish Inquisition and raises a little girl back to life in front of the cathedral. Just as the crowd shout his praises the Grand Inquisitor himself rides past and orders his men to arrest and imprison Jesus. That night he comes to Jesus in his cell, to tell him that since he has come to hinder the Inquisition and the Catholic Church he will be burnt at the stake the next day.

The Grand Inquisitor mockingly interrogates Jesus, taunting him with his threefold temptations in the desert. He tells Jesus that he should have turned the stones to bread, for then he could have fed the crowds and won their unthinking and undying loyalty; he should have jumped off the pinnacle of the temple, for the miracle would have dazzled the crowds into accepting his claims; finally, he should have accepted Satan's offer of all the kingdoms of the world.

On behalf of the church the Grand Inquisitor confesses, "Just eight centuries ago, we took from him what You rejected with scorn, that last gift he offered You, showing You all the kingdoms of the earth. We took from him Rome and the sword of Caesar, and proclaimed ourselves sole rulers of the earth." He goes on, "If you had taken the world and Caesar's purple, you would have founded the universal state and have given universal peace."[2]

If only Jesus had taken Caesar's purple he could have founded one great empire to rule the whole world! Truth would have died, the hope of freedom would have perished, and the kingdoms of this world could have continued as they always had.

Jesus listens attentively, his gentle eyes lovingly watching the Grand Inquisitor, but he refuses to speak. The Grand Inquisitor longs for him to say something, but after a prolonged silence Jesus suddenly approaches the old man and softly kisses him on his bloodless, aged lips. The Grand Inquisitor opens the door and lets Jesus go. Dostoyevsky's account ends with Jesus's kiss glowing in the old man's heart – and yet he stubbornly refuses to change his ways.

Just as Jesus rejected Satan's temptation to prostrate himself in order to gain "all the kingdoms of the world" and "their glory" (Luke 4:5–6), so the early church spurned Caesar's sword and purple, the symbols of power and honour. Instead, they followed the example of Jesus and Paul, living pure lives and serving in holiness and humility. Only after Constantine did church leaders begin wearing purple and behaving like high government officials rather than agents of the countercultural kingdom of God. The church gained wealth and prestige, but lost the spiritual power and authority that characterized the ministry of Jesus and the early Christian leaders. The church became like the world, adopting its values rather than transforming the world by dethroning its godless mindset through love, truth and sacrifice. Ultimately, like the Grand Inquisitor, the church found itself opposing the gospel and the Spirit.

Christian leaders today are confronted with the same temptation. When we use our positions to gain honour for ourselves we betray the gospel; and the churches we lead – which should be beacons of light in a dark world –

---

2. Fyodor Dostoyevsky, *The Gospel in Dostoyevsky* (Farmington, PA: Plough Publishing, 1988), 33.

become stumbling blocks to outsiders watching us. In this era of unprecedented openness to Christ throughout much of the Middle East, it is imperative that church leaders adopt a Jesus-centred understanding of authority. In this book, I have focused on the Muslim world; but the growing churches in East Asia, Africa and Latin America will also need to move beyond the domineering model of leadership if they are to realize their transformative potential for their societies. The declining churches of Europe and North America can experience renewal as their leaders let go of the respectability they used to enjoy in the past, and recommit themselves to being countercultural agents of the Kingdom of God.

In the face of this challenge, do we harden our hearts like the Grand Inquisitor? Do we hang on to the power, prestige and perks of our positions? Dare we let go of this world's pomp, that we may see the true glory of God's kingdom? May the Lord give us grace to follow Jesus, giving up the purple and embracing the shame – just as Paul did – that we may receive the greatest honour and joy of hearing his "Well done!"

Langham Literature and its imprints are a ministry of Langham Partnership.

Langham Partnership is a global fellowship working in pursuit of the vision God entrusted to its founder John Stott –

> *to facilitate the growth of the church in maturity and Christ-likeness through raising the standards of biblical preaching and teaching.*

Our vision is to see churches in the majority world equipped for mission and growing to maturity in Christ through the ministry of pastors and leaders who believe, teach and live by the Word of God.

Our mission is to strengthen the ministry of the Word of God through:
- nurturing national movements for biblical preaching
- fostering the creation and distribution of evangelical literature
- enhancing evangelical theological education

especially in countries where churches are under-resourced.

Our ministry

Langham Preaching partners with national leaders to nurture indigenous biblical preaching movements for pastors and lay preachers all around the world. With the support of a team of trainers from many countries, a multi-level programme of seminars provides practical training, and is followed by a programme for training local facilitators. Local preachers' groups and national and regional networks ensure continuity and ongoing development, seeking to build vigorous movements committed to Bible exposition.

Langham Literature provides majority world preachers, scholars and seminary libraries with evangelical books and electronic resources through publishing and distribution, grants and discounts. The programme also fosters the creation of indigenous evangelical books in many languages, through writer's grants, strengthening local evangelical publishing houses, and investment in major regional literature projects, such as one volume Bible commentaries like *The Africa Bible Commentary* and *The South Asia Bible Commentary*.

Langham Scholars provides financial support for evangelical doctoral students from the majority world so that, when they return home, they may train pastors and other Christian leaders with sound, biblical and theological teaching. This programme equips those who equip others. Langham Scholars also works in partnership with majority world seminaries in strengthening evangelical theological education. A growing number of Langham Scholars study in high quality doctoral programmes in the majority world itself. As well as teaching the next generation of pastors, graduated Langham Scholars exercise significant influence through their writing and leadership.

To learn more about Langham Partnership and the work we do visit **langham.org**

Lightning Source UK Ltd.
Milton Keynes UK
UKHW021130070920
369492UK00016B/1140

9 781783 686810